Sexual Perversion
Integrative Treatment Approaches
for the Clinician

Sexual Perversion
Integrative Treatment Approaches for the Clinician

Sheldon Travin, M.D.
Bronx-Lebanon Hospital Center and
Albert Einstein College of Medicine
New York, New York

and
Barry Protter, Ph.D.
William Alanson White Institute of Psychoanalysis and
Albert Einstein College of Medicine
New York, New York

Plenum Press • New York and London

Library of Congress Cataloging-in-Publication Data

```
Travin, Sheldon.
    Sexual perversion : integrative treatment approaches for the
  clinician / Sheldon Travin and Barry Protter.
       p.   cm.
    Includes bibliographical references and index.
    ISBN 0-306-44380-5
    1. Sexual deviation.   I. Protter, Barry.  II. Title.
    [DNLM: 1. Paraphilias--therapy.   WM 610 T782s]
  RC556.T725  1993
  616.85'83--dc20
  DNLM/DLC
  for Library of Congress                              92-49113
                                                           CIP
```

ISBN 0-306-44380-5

© 1993 Plenum Press, New York
A Division of Plenum Publishing Corporation
233 Spring Street, New York, N.Y. 10013

All rights reserved

No part of this book may be reproduced, stored in a retrieval system, or transmitted in any form or by any means, electronic, mechanical, photocopying, microfilming, recording, or otherwise, without written permission from the Publisher

Printed in the United States of America

Preface

This book represents the distillation of our experiences in treating individuals suffering from a variety of sexual perversions. As mental health practitioners, we have encountered from the very beginning of our professional lives patients who manifested some of the milder forms of sexual perversions. These therapeutic contacts have taken place in a number of different settings and were informed by a primarily psychodynamic perspective, inasmuch as both authors have had formal postgraduate psychoanalytic training.

At a later juncture in our careers we became specialists in the areas of forensic psychiatry (S.T.) and forensic psychology (B.P.), respectively. Within this context we had on numerous occasions evaluated sexual acting-out disorders for the criminal justice system.

Approximately nine years ago we became involved in the specialized assessment and treatment of sex offenders at the Sex Offender Treatment Program of the Bronx-Lebanon Hospital Court Clinic. This program has a primarily cognitive-behavioral orientation. As a result of these varied experiences, we have increasingly made ourselves available for private consultation and treatment of a wide range of paraphiliac disorders. It is from this diverse background of clinical settings and experiences that we have attempted to integrate key sensibilities from the behavioral and psychodynamic perspectives and to construct a core bimodal treatment approach, which also incorporates other treatment perspectives.

We wish to thank Harvey Bluestone, Director of Psychiatry at Bronx-Lebanon Hospital Center, for his continued support and particularly for his guidance in treating these difficult patients at the Sex Offender Treatment Program. Special thanks are also due to Ken Cullen for his contributions in treating sex offenders at the Court Clinic. We also wish to express our appreciation to Beth Langan for her editorial assistance.

Contents

Introduction 11

References 15

Chapter 1
A Brief History of Sexual Perversion 17

Premodern Perspectives 18
Modern Perspectives 21
Descriptive Medico-Psychiatric Approach 22
Sexologic Approach 23
Psychoanalytic Approach 26
Psychotechnologic Approach 27
Sociopolitical Approach 28
Modern Legal-Forensic Considerations 30
Conclusion 32
References 33

Chapter 2
The Prevalence of Sexual Perversion 37

Criminologic Data on Sexual Assaults 38
Clinical Perspectives on Prevalence 43
Survey Data on Sexual Abuse 49

Conclusion 54
References 55

Chapter 3
The Diagnosis and Classification of Sexual Perversion 59

Psychiatric Diagnoses of Sexual Perversions 60
Typological and Classificatory Considerations 65
Personality Factors in Sexual Perversions 67
Conclusion 69
References 70

Chapter 4
Biological Perspectives on Sexual Perversion 73

Biological Factors in Gender Development 73
Plasma Testosterone Levels and Sexual Aggression 78
Brain Damage, Dysfunction, and Temporal Lobe Disorders 80
Alcohol and Sexual Assault 83
Depression, Obsessive-Compulsive Disorder, Paraphilia, and
    Nonparaphiliac Sexual Addiction 84
Conclusion 86
References 86

Chapter 5
Behavioral and Cognitive View on Sexual Perversion 91

Models of Learning Behavior 91
Cognition and Behavior 95
Discussion 97
References 98

Chapter 6
Psychodynamic Perspectives of Sexual Perversion 101

Review of Psychodynamic Formulations 101
    Classical and Revisionistic Views 101
    Relational Schools 107

Contemporary Pluralistic Outlook 109
Brief Comments on Specific Perversions 111
Brief Note on Incest 114
Fantasy and Sexual Perversion 115
Conclusion 116
References 117

Chapter 7
The Assessment of Sexual Perversion **121**

Comprehensive Psychiatric Interview 122
Detailed Sexual Interview 124
Psychodynamic Formulation 127
Specialized Psychological Testing 128
Penile Plethysmographic Assessment 129
Conclusion 131
References 132

Chapter 8
The Treatment of Sexual Perversion **135**

Psychodynamic Approaches to Perversion 136
Cognitive-Behavioral Approaches to Perversion 141
    Self-Control Techniques 142
    Stress Management 144
    Cognitive Restructuring 145
    Social Rehabilitative Techniques 145
    Sex Education 146
Relapse Prevention with Sexual Perversion 147
Organic Approaches to Sexual Perversion 149
Family Systems Approach to Sexual Perversion 150
Conclusion 152
References 153

Chapter 9
Integrative Perspectives on Treating Sexual Perversion **155**

Bimodal Approach to Treatment 157
Cognitive-Behavioral Component 158

Focused Psychodynamic Component 159
Multimodal Integration 161
References 162

Chapter 10
Clinical Applications of Treatment: Integrative Approaches .. 163

The Severe Paraphiliac Patient 164
    Specialized Treatment Program 165
    Private Practice Referral 167
    Disclosure in Psychotherapy 174
The Moderate Paraphiliac Patient 178
The Mild Paraphiliac Patient 185
The Transient Sexually Perverse Experience 189
The Compulsive Nonparaphiliac Sexually Disordered Patient 190
Female Sexual Perversions 191
References 193

Chapter 11
Summary and Conclusion 195

Index 199

Introduction

The title of this book, *Sexual Perversion: Integrative Treatment Approaches for the Clinician*, is purposefully problematic. It highlights the extraordinary ambiguity that envelops discussions of individuals whose conviction and/or diagnosis identify them as sick and/or criminal, and in announcing its stance (treating), as well as in naming its subject (the sexually perverse patient), it necessarily evokes a medical/social/legal history fraught with prejudice, misunderstanding, and downright hostility. To this day, each of the terms in the book's title generates heated controversy not only as to definition, but also as to the very legitimacy of this domain of scientific inquiry.

Although the term "sexual perversion" has a pejorative connotation, it conveys a sense of historical perspective to the subject. Throughout history, various sexual activities have been labeled by different societies as immoral, unnatural, and wicked; in short, "perverse." *Webster's New World Dictionary* defines "perverse" as "deviating from what is considered right or good; wrong, improper etc. or corrupt, wicked ... "[1] (p 1009). Although the pejorative connotations of the term "paraphilia" used for sexually deviant behavior in the *Diagnostic and Statistical Manual of Mental Disorders* of the American Psychiatric Association (DSM-III-R)[2] may not be as readily apparent, they exist nonetheless, as can be seen in Webster's definition of the prefix "para" as in medicine, "functionally disordered abnormal ... "[1] (p 978). Given these similarities of meaning, we have chosen to use the term "sexual perversion" for several reasons. As Stoller says, "perversion is a sturdy word, throbbing with assumptions, while paraphilia is a wet noodle"[3] (p 6). Moreover, historically, depth-psychological approaches to this topic use the term "perversion" as pioneered by Freud in his investigations of unconscious desire and psychic reality. Because we will be reviewing intrapsychic processes relating to deviant sexual behavior, the term perversion seems to be appropriate.

What then constitutes the sexually perverse patient? Some would argue that elements of perverse sexuality are universal features of human nature, which stem from an archaic developmental past. Each individual has the potential to at least transiently fantasize sexually perverse activities. Perverse fantasies, and in some instances perverse behavior, can be found in any individual and indeed, may be seen in a wide range of patients that one encounters in a general psychotherapeutic practice. On the other hand, there are individuals who are consumed by sexually perverse fantasies and behaviors; the most extreme cases of these are those individuals whose sexual activities infringe on the rights of others. Individuals who engage in this kind of unlawful sexual behavior can be categorized as sexual abusers, and if legally apprehended, assume the status of the so-called "sex offenders." In the literature, these two groups—the non–acting-out patients with mild and occasionally perverse inclinations, and the more compulsive perverse individuals who abuse and offend—are discussed in different categories. Both from a theoretical and from a treatment perspective, there are pragmatic advantages that encourage many professionals to see these two groups as distinct. Although individuals in the more "benign" group may present symptoms in the context of other psychological manifestations, they are self-referred in the traditional clinical way, whereas those individuals in the compulsively acting-out group tend to become patients (often reluctantly) only when forced to by third-party influence with legal leverage.

Although it may be accurate to say that the former group merely evidences perverse symptomatology, while the latter group is diagnosable as a paraphiliac disorder, we believe that this bifurcation unnecessarily and overly constricts discussions of the

Introduction

complexities of clinically treating perverse sexuality. The authors, having treated both populations in private and in forensic clinical settings, will thus bring to bear on this topic a cross-fertilization of sensibilities gleaned from their experiences. Although we certainly recognize the profound distinction, both clinical and theoretical, between the narcissistic patient, who has mildly upsetting sadomasochistic fantasies and the acting-out pedophile, nevertheless, we feel that there is much to be gained by integrating the concerns typically considered unique to each group. On the one hand, those psychotherapists who treat the more "benign" perverse patients and are likely to be working from a more dynamic, existential, and humanistic stance, need to be sensitized to clinical behavioral self-control issues, third-party legal consequences, and ethical concerns inherent in this area. On the other hand, those specialists treating sex offenders, while rightly concerned with behavioral self-control and ethical-forensic matters, can enhance their overall effectiveness by appreciating the deeply embedded nature of perversion in character formation and the nuances of interpersonal relationships.

Whatever the severity of the individual's perverse behavior, and regardless of the situation where the individual is encountered (private office or institutional setting), one needs to recognize that the treatment of all variants of "normative" sexual behavior is profoundly embedded in the social, moral, cultural, historical, and political contexts within which perverse behavior is defined and understood. One only has to consider the recent mental health debates about definitions of homosexuality to appreciate the impact sociopolitical considerations and conventions have in defining patienthood status in the realm of deviant psychosexual disturbance.[4] There is no question that sociocultural factors have influenced, if not constituted, the judgments of what is considered normative and what is labeled sexually perverse. We should also be reminded that at one time oral sex was considered to be a sexually perverse activity and around the turn of the century masturbation was believed to be the biological basis of many sexual perversions.[5]

Furthermore, the notion that individuals suffering from sexual perversions should be treated as patients is a relatively modern concept that still generates its share of controversy. Again, the political-moral dimension often becomes a paramount issue with this treatment population. From the moralistic right, we hear expressions of outrage and a fervor to punish many of these individuals. This fervor is exemplified by the recent dramatic publicity focused on child sexual abuse, accompanied by demands in many quarters for stiffer penalties for sexual offenders. From the sexual politics of the left, there are critics of the mental health establishment's attempts to diagnose and treat deviant sexual disorders. These critics, among whom are various sexual minority rights groups, advocate the right to be different and free in their sexual expression without being labeled as "sick"; many of them excoriate the mental health professional's role as a social control agent.

Even those psychotherapists who are generally sympathetic to the notion of treating sexual perversions tend to be willing to treat victimless deviant sexually disordered patients such as fetishists, but are understandably reluctant to treat patients suffering from paraphiliac disorders (such as pedophiles), who sexually violate victims. This reluctance raises issues of countertransference, excessive concerns about third-party liability, and the need in some instances for the psychotherapist to work with third-party agencies such as the probation department and courts. These latter concerns loom particularly large because they go against the traditional dyadic therapist–patient model of confidentiality. Psychotherapists' disinclination to get involved in a treatment situation with potentially harmful paraphiliac-disordered patients may be reflected in the often-expressed skepticism of treatment outcome in this admittedly difficult population.

In summary, treating sexually perverse patients is so enmeshed with sociocultural, moral, ethical, legal, and political considerations as to require the clinician to draw upon a diversity of perspectives and skills in order to be effective and to achieve a degree of professional competence in working with these patients. The purpose of this book is to present a comprehensive overview of the cardinal issues involved in treating sexually perverse patients. In view of the complex nature of these disorders, the conditions under which the patients are seen, and the social context in which the psychotherapist functions, it is essential that the psychotherapist be aware of, and be able to utilize, various resources in a multimodal perspective for effective treatment. This book therefore advocates an integrative approach to treatment. It is written for general psychotherapists who may encounter sexually perverse patients in their practices, as well as for those sexual therapists who specialize in this area.

REFERENCES

1. Neufeld V, Guralnik DB, eds. *Webster's New World Dictionary of American English.* Third College Edition. New York, NY: Simon & Schuster; 1991.
2. American Psychiatric Association. *Diagnostic and Statistical Manual of Mental Disorders (DSM-III-R).* 3rd ed, revised. Washington, DC: American Psychiatric Association; 1987.
3. Stoller RJ. Observing the Erotic Imagination. New Haven, Conn: Yale University Press; 1985.
4. Bayer R. *Homosexuality and American Psychiatry. The Politics of Diagnosis.* Princeton, NJ: Princeton University Press; 1987.
5. Engelhardt JHT. The disease of masturbation: values and the concept of disease. Bull Hist Med. 1974; 48:234–248.

1

A Brief History of Sexual Perversion

The history of perversions essentially constitutes a subtext of the larger history of sexuality; the two are intimately intertwined. Despite the apparent impact of societal attitudes on sexuality throughout the ages, the study of human sexuality has been a subject largely ignored by historians. Only in recent years has sexuality become a subject of serious study.[1] Historically, perversion has been the dark side of sexuality that was itself already shrouded in a repressive silence and taboo. Viewed as the unspeakable incarnation of evil, perverse sexual behavior has been considered sinful, blasphemous, immoral, corrupt, and illegal—in fact, as a crime calling for severe punitive measures. In more recent times, it has been perceived as incorrigibly abnormal, pathological, a loathsome disease unvarying in its relentless downward course. Even so respected a pioneer as Krafft-Ebing,[2] in his work on perversion, initially published the descriptions of sexual acts in Latin, in part because of the likelihood of societal outrage at the time. Only in the past half-century or so has a slowly evolving change emerged in attitudes toward perverse sexuality.

For purpose of explication, the history of perversion can be viewed from two main perspectives—premodern and modern. In using these terms for our discussion of perverse sexuality, we are following Robinson's[3] use of these terms in his narrative on human sexuality. The premodern perspective represents the history of perversion before it became a domain of scientific classification and study appropriated by a multitude of specialists. In the premodern perspective, the history of perversion must be traced within an array of traditions: religious, mythological, cultural, literary, and legal. The modern perspective, which emerges approximately in the mid-nineteenth century, involves disciplines such as anthropology, medicine, psychiatry, psychoanalysis, and sexology; thus, from the modern perspective, any discussion of perversion necessarily acknowledges a range of considerations that include the emerging "psychotechnologic," sociopolitical, and legal-forensic aspects.

PREMODERN PERSPECTIVES

In his comprehensive 1976 history of *Sexual Variance in Society and History*, Bullough[4] outlines the main prescientific traditions in the area of variant sexuality. Bullough describes the early biblical sources of ancient judaism as proscribing such sexual activities as homosexuality, bestiality, transvestism, and masturbation. On the other hand, he notes that the ancient Greeks had a more tolerant view of most sexual activities, providing they did not threaten the integrity of the family. Homosexuality was pervasive: men impersonated women in the theater; cross-dressing occurred at Dionysius' festivals; sadomasochistic practices were incorporated in certain religious ceremonies; bestiality was described in fables and romances; and a sexual relationship between an adult male and a young boy was considered a respected form of education. Licht[5] points out, however, that to the Greeks a "young boy" actually meant a sexually mature or pubescent male. Furthermore, the sensual part of the relationship was not necessarily the most significant. Rather, for the Greeks, this love of boys "has its roots in the unexampled ethical valuation of the masculine character in public and private life"[6] (p 440). The term "pederasty" comes from the Greek "boy" and "love"; in ancient Greece, this term had absolutely no pejorative connotation. This attitude toward pederasty seems to have passed on to the early Romans, as the behavior was quite common. Julius Caesar, the founder of the Empire, who was sexually active with women, was also a practicing homosexual.[7] Given this context, early Christianity was viewed as a sex-negative religion which condemned all forms of sex other than for the purpose of procreation, and limited even procreative sex by defining the form it must take: the male in the top position and the female on her back. The church labeled any other kind of sexual activity as sinful; eventually, sexual activity that deviated from this prescribed pattern came to be considered bizarre or perverted.[7] Augustine, who influenced much of this thinking, believed that "sex after the Fall is evil primarily because it interferes with... the peace of scholarship and meditation"[8] (p 48). He advocated total abstinence as the best course, but qualified this radical position by suggesting that men who could not achieve perfect abstinence should marry. Marriage, for Augustine, had three main duties: procreation, fidelity, and sacrament. The extent to which definitions of sexual perversion are relative can be glimpsed by contrasting Augustine's position with that of medieval Islam, which was relatively lenient toward such practices as homosexuality, bestiality, transvestism, and anal intercourse.[4] In the West, the Early Middle Ages essentially extended the older injunctions against nonprocreative sex. The only form of deviant sexual activity which seems to have been tolerated to some degree was female transvestism, possibly as a manifestation of the superior role of man. Later medieval attitudes toward deviant sexual practices were characterized by contradictions: although these practices were ostensibly condemned as heresy, and offenders punished, some institutions encouraging these behaviors were tolerated. Sussman[9] describes periods of shifting attitudes toward sexuality and morality in England culminating by 1840 in the firm establishment of Victorianism, the predominant sexual motif of which was denial and repression. Masturbation was almost an obsession with Victorians, who, influenced by warnings from the urologist William Acton, believed masturbation caused a variety of disastrous consequences. Behind the Victorian facade, however, there appears to have existed an extensive sexual subculture, reflected in the high percentage of illegitimate births, the prevalence of prostitution, volumes of pornography (including the suggestively titled *My Secret Life* published anonymously by a Victorian gentleman), and periodic sex scandals. One famous example of a Victorian secret life is Queen Victoria's Prime Minister, William Gladstone. The publication of Gladstone's diary in 1975 revealed that, between the years 1840 and 1854, this politically powerful and socially eminent advisor to the Queen both frequented brothels and flagellated himself. Nor was Gladstone unique; flagellation, considered on the Continent to be the English vice, was widely portrayed in the arts and was a not uncommon practice in the sexually repressed society of Victorian England. The colonial American outlook toward sex, summarized by Bullough,[4] was significantly influenced by Puritanism, and nonprocreative sex of any kind was condemned, particularly, homosexuality. This attitude continued into the postrevolutionary era.

When we turn to literature, two names are notably associated with perversion: the Marquis de Sade and Leopold Von Sacher-Masoch. Donatien-Alphonse-François, the Marquis de Sade, was born into a line of French nobility on June 2, 1740, and was repeatedly imprisoned for sexually scandalous behavior.[10] Among his major works, many of them written during the half of his adult life that he spent imprisoned or confined to insane asylums, were *One Hundred and Twenty Days of Sodom, The Adversities of Virtue, Justine, and Juliette*. In these writings, de Sade depicts in graphic detail such sadistic forms of perverse behavior as floggings, tortures, and mutilations of women. In 1803, de Sade was transferred to Charenton insane asylum where he managed for a time to stage theatrical performances of his plays and where he eventually died on December 2, 1814. Napoleon himself, offended by de Sade's attack on him and Josephine in a piece titled *Zoloe et ses Deux Acolytes*[10] (and presumably by his other writings and sexual behavior as well), personally ensured that de Sade be deprived of all freedom of movement.[11] Gonzalez-Crussi[12] believes that Napoleon wanted this man whom he considered dangerous to be denied not only freedom of movement, but also freedom of expression. Although it is doubtful whether anybody really considered de Sade to be incurably insane, there appeared to be a consensus about the need to have him permanently removed from society for its own protection. Leopold von Sacher-

Masoch, born in Galicia on January 27, 1836, was an Austrian writer who achieved moderate fame for his portrayal of life in his native land before becoming increasingly involved in writing about sensual and perverse themes.[10] His most popular novel, *Venus in Furs*, published in 1870, depicts in exquisite detail the subjugation and humiliation of the main male character, Severin, by a dominating tormentress, who, clothed in furs and boots, wields a whip. Krafft-Ebing,[2] familiar with the writings of these two authors, coined the terms "sadism" and "masochism" to describe perverse sexual behavior associated with pleasure derived from inflicting pain in sadism and from suffering pain or subjugation in masochism.

In regard to legal attitudes toward deviant sexual practices, early punitive measures were extremely harsh.[4] For example, prior to the Revolution in France, a conviction of sodomy in that country could result in being condemned to death by burning. This harshness was modified with the implementation of the Napoleonic Code in 1810, which treated deviant sexual acts as crimes only when these acts outraged public decency, involved violence, or lacked valid consent (for example, by involving an adult and an underage individual). The Napoleonic legal code was adopted and/or adapted by many countries in Continental Europe, with the notable exception of England, which had been influenced earlier by Sir William Blackstone's idea that even if both parties consented to a sex act "against nature," both should be liable to be prosecuted.

MODERN PERSPECTIVES

Modern attempts to study perverse sexual behavior in a systematic manner can be essentially categorized into five major historical currents. The first of these, which we can call the *descriptive medico-psychiatric* approach, was initiated in the latter part of the nineteenth century. The second and third categories—the *sexologic* and the *psychoanalytic* approaches, respectively—began largely in the early part of the twentieth century and are still flourishing. The fourth category, which we term the *psy-*

chotechnologic, makes use of the newer technologies, including behavioral and learning techniques and physiologically based procedures that have been rapidly developing in the past couple of decades. The fifth category, the *sociopolitical,* has assumed increasing significance in the last quarter of a century, and overlaps with modern legal-forensic considerations.

DESCRIPTIVE MEDICO-PSYCHIATRIC APPROACH

The landmark study of sexual perversions is Richard von Krafft-Ebing's *Psychopathia Sexualis,*[2] published in 1886. In this book, Krafft-Ebing describes a wide array of deviant sexual cases, ranging from clothing fetishisms to grisly sadistic mutilations, which he had collected during his years of forensic work with the courts. The perverse acts that Krafft-Ebing described were grouped together indiscriminately, the relatively minor deviations with the most heinous ones involving extreme violence directed at the victims. Krafft-Ebing believed these sexually perverse behaviors stemmed from hereditary predispositions, and were manifestations of incurable disease processes, often brought on by such factors as the excessive onanism he found in characters displaying moral turpitude. Although Krafft-Ebing was a pioneer in the descriptive delineation of sexually deviant behaviors including homosexuality, and thus paved the way for further discussion on this heretofore largely neglected area, there were serious errors in his work. His identification of masturbation as a causal factor in all sexual deviations, including homosexuality and lust murder,[13] as well as his descriptions of the entire array of deviant sexual behaviors in close proximity with each other, left indelible (and unfortunate) impressions in the minds of readers. The influence of Krafft-Ebing's work on descriptive psychiatry, the mental health establishment, and society in general has been profound. It should be pointed out that Krafft-Ebing was Professor of Psychiatry at the University of Vienna—a position of enormous professional prestige; he was, in fact, one of the three influential academicians who had helped Sigmund Freud achieve the rank of Associate Professor at the University.[14] Consequently, only relatively recently have there been attempts to extricate the useful information he amassed from the generally pessimistic indiscriminating notions that informed his study of perversion. These attempts have become possible because of the recognition that such notions as a morally degenerative character and an incurably degenerative process, are intrinsic not merely to Krafft-Ebing's subject but to the archaic medical model within which he worked.

SEXOLOGIC APPROACH

The attempt to study the entire panoply of sexual behavior without limiting its scope to a disease entity, brought about the loosely defined discipline of so-called sexology. This perspective tended to humanize the attitude of the scientific community and the public at large toward the variety of sexual expression. In Germany, Magnus Hirschfeld founded the Institute of Sexual Science in Berlin in 1918. He wrote extensively about human sexuality, especially about sexual anomalies such as homosexuality, sadomasochism, fetishism, and exhibitionism, and he coined such terms as "transvestism" to depict cross-dressing. Most importantly, Hirschfeld underscored the connection between the action of hormones and the development of human sexuality in his theory of sexual phases. In fact, he attributed all sexual anomalies to irregularities in development. But instead of "rejecting the theory of psychophysical parallelism,"[15] (p XIV) Hirschfeld actually "applied the results of the psychoanalytic school to sexual anomalies of physiological origin" (p XIV). The major figure in sexology in England was Henry Havelock Ellis, whose long life spanned the last of the nineteenth century and the first three decades of the twentieth century. Robinson[3] unequivocally considers Ellis to have been the supreme figure in the emerging modern sexual ethos. Brecher[13] describes how Ellis, during his adolescence, did not masturbate but instead began to experience copious seminal emissions during sleep, without any sensation of orgasm, at least once a week. This was a source of considerable dread for him because "spermatorrhea," or involuntary seminal discharges, was believed to cause a wide range of progressive diseases. Having thus experienced the miseries of sexual misinformation and repression, perhaps inherent in a Victorian childhood, Ellis resolved to become a medical doctor—not to practice, but to acquire the scientific experience to study sex. Ellis' masterwork, *Studies in the Psychology of Sex*,[16] was published first in German in 1896 and then in English in 1897. Ellis continued to revise and expand this work until he published the 1936 version, which consisted of a total of thirty-two studies. These studies have formed much of the basis of the modern view of human sexuality. A few of his many findings illustrate the extent to which Ellis' work made possible the emergence of a modern view of sexuality. Sexual behavior and sexual responses often appear at a very early age, Ellis asserted, and masturbation is a common phenomenon at all ages in both males and females. Equally significant was his finding that "homosexuality and heterosexuality are not absolutes like black and white; they are present in varying degrees..."[13] (p 37). Although his studies were criticized as being largely impressionistic and anecdotal, he nevertheless made a tremendous contribution in regard to sexual deviation by lifting it out of the moralistic and narrowly legalistic framework to which it had previously been consigned. By accepting as naturalistic and benign such variants of human sexuality as masturbation and homosexuality, which had been judged as either perverse, sick, or criminal by his predecessors, Ellis, in effect, situated human sexual experience within a more relativistic framework. He can, therefore, be seen as a great pioneering influence in the move toward sexual enlightenment and the reshaping of sexual attitudes that has taken place in the last quarter century in the Western world.

No attempts to discuss sexology can possibly be undertaken without emphasizing the monumental contributions made by Kinsey and his associates in their investigations into human sexual behavior. When Alfred Kinsey, Professor of Zoology at Indiana University, was asked in 1938 to coordinate a marriage course to be given to students at the University, Kinsey discovered that there was a paucity of adequate research in the field.[17] Falling back on his previous experience in systematically collecting biological data on gall wasp insects, Kinsey set out to learn firsthand as much as he could about sexual behavior. By conducting personal interviews, Kinsey was able to obtain 350 sexual histories of his students in the first year. Kinsey continued to refine his interviewing protocol until it included a minimum of 350 and a maximum of 521 items. Kinsey and his associates provided details of the interviewing technique in Chapter 2 of *Sexual Behavior in the Human Male*,[18] published in 1948, that presented data obtained from 5300 white males. In 1953, *Sexual Behavior in the Human Female*[19] was published. This work contained the statistically analyzed data obtained from 5940 white females. Kinsey and his associates thus provided the essential reference point for all subsequent attempts to obtain systematic data on the broad spectrum of human sexuality. Unlike any previous studies, Kinsey's work elicited responses to explicit questions aimed at specific types of sexual experiences and their frequency of occurrences. These findings indicated that a number of sexual activities previously considered "marginal"—including fellatio and cunnilingus, as well as extramarital and homosexual encounters—were more pervasive than it had been acknowledged. Indeed, these findings led the authors to insist that heterosexuality and homosexuality did not represent two discrete behavioral patterns.[18] Instead, they argued, mixtures of heterosexual–homosexual experiences could be described as occurring on a continuum, with a rating scale from 0 (exclusively heterosexual) to 6 (exclusively homosexual), depending on the relative amounts of each activity in the individual. Among the findings with which Kinsey riveted the American public's attention and revolutionized our knowledge of sexual behavior were the following: (1) approximately 37% of the males have some homosexual encounter leading to orgasm between adolescence and old age, (2) approximately 8% of the males are exclusively homosexual, and (3) approximately 50% of the males never have any homosexual experiences after adolescence. Given his findings, the effect of Kinsey's work has been to legitimize sexual variability. Kinsey and his associates went on to interview sex offenders in prison. After Kinsey's death in 1956, the work was continued by Gebhard and other members of the Institute for Sex Research at Indiana University. The number of persons ultimately interviewed in this study was 1356 white male sex offenders accounting for 2274 sex offenses, 888 white males in prison, and 477 white males in a control group. The results of this study were published in 1965 as *Sex Offenders: An Analysis of Types*. Gebhard and his associates[20] had attempted to compare sex offenders, prison groups, and control groups in regard to a number of selected items. In their examinations, the researchers found that particular types of sex offenders could be further classified into subtypes having certain variables of behavior. However, some of these variables were also found among the prison group, and therefore were not unique to sex offenders.

PSYCHOANALYTIC APPROACH

Sigmund Freud, the founder of psychoanalysis, viewed sexuality, in the broad sense of the term, as central to human nature and to psychic disturbance. His investigations represent the first in-depth studies of sexuality, probing into such matters as its early developmental phases, transformations, and the etiological significance of a variety of psychological phenomena. In *Three Essays on the Theory of Sexuality*,[21] Freud described perversion as developmentally normal for the infant—as a polymorphous perverse manifestation of exaggerated pregenital activities of a not yet fully formed and integrated sexuality. Perversions were, therefore, carry-overs of component infantile sexual activities that had not been fully integrated with other psychic structures and the demands of reality in adulthood. Freud's contributions were groundbreaking in placing perversions within the natural developmental history of the individual. By offering a treatment context in which these disorders could be approached, he made a monumental leap forward from earlier descriptive accounts of perversion as a vaguely though essentially morally tinged, incurable disease process.

Subsequent post-Freudian developments in psychoanalysis have expanded upon and modified various aspects of Freud's conceptualizations of perversion, particularly his emphasis on the role of instincts. Such central facets of human experience as the need for relatedness and the formation of self and identity came to be seen as playing the more primary role in the formation of perversions. As a result, post-Freudian treatment perspectives have been modified in orientation.

PSYCHOTECHNOLOGIC APPROACH

In the past quarter of the century, there have been attempts to employ specialized assessment and treatment techniques in the area of human sexuality. These new technologies make use of behavioral techniques, learning theory, and physiological methods. The emphasis is on obtaining objective data by monitoring observable and measurable sexual responses and activities. According to Pomeroy,[17] Kinsey had hoped to gain firsthand knowledge about a wide range of sexual activities, but because his research group tended to be extremely cautious, they missed many opportunities. The data they did accumulate on human sexual anatomy and physiology were incorporated in the chapters "Anatomy of Sexual Response and Orgasm" and "Physiology of Sexual Response and Orgasm" in their volume on female behavior. Pomeroy goes on to point out that, by directly observing a limited number of human sexual activities and recording them on film, Kinsey essentially anticipated the subsequent physiological research of Masters and Johnson, who were able to persevere and thus make a monumental contribution to our knowledge of human sexuality. By directly observing and recording the physiological reactions in human males and females to sexual stimulation, they were able to amass crucial data on basic physiological facts. The results of their studies were published in their book *Human Sexual Response*,[22] in 1966. Fours year later, Masters and Johnson published a second book, *Human Sexual Inadequacy*.[23] In this work, they described the use of basic psychophysiological processes for innovative therapeutic procedures, including the treatment of both sexual partners by a dual therapy team for such sexual disorders as premature ejaculation, impotence, and orgasmic dysfunction.

This emphasis on obtaining data has carried over to the area of sexually deviant behavior. The accuracy and utility of the clinical assessment of the patient's deviant sexual behavior by self-report during the interview have been expanded by having the patient complete special scales, questionnaires, and inventories pertaining to deviant sexual fantasy and behavior. Most prominent among the new technologies is the increasing use of erection measurement responses to deviant sexual stimuli in the laboratory setting—a technology that owes much to the innovative work of Freund in the 1950s and 1960s.[24] Treatment techniques have included self-control, aversive, and cognitive rehabilitative interventions that have been drawn from a variety of cognitive-behavioral treatment paradigms, many of them employed in a group therapy format.[25]

Although there is no conclusive evidence linking elevated plasma testosterone levels with deviant sexual behavior, androgen-depleting agents, such as medroxyprogesterone acetate (MPA, Depo-Provera), have been used to decrease the plasma testosterone of sexual deviants from the male to the female level, which has been correlated with diminished sexual drive.[26] Currently, some researchers are experimenting with combining androgen-depleting agents with cognitive-behavioral treatment, and, as the present authors recommend in selected cases, with psychodynamic approaches in an integrated, multimodal model. The focus of treatment is to help patients gain control over, if not entirely overcome, their deviant sexual urges.

SOCIOPOLITICAL APPROACH

Whereas the psychoanalytic tradition attempted to explain sexually perverse behavior as a derivative of underlying individual unconscious processes, the more recent psychosociologic investigations focus on the underlying social and political dynamics as contributing to the manifestations of perverse behavior, as well as on the processes involved in labeling what is normal and what is perverse. Chasseguet-Smirgel[27] has written about the "perverse core latent within each one of us that is capable of being activated under certain circumstances" (p 1). She emphasizes that "perversion and perverse behavior are particularly present at those times in the history of mankind which precede or accompany major social and political upheavals" (p 1). Historically, certain societies (ie, Nazi Germany) have legitimized sadistic practices and encouraged individuals with such propensities to express them under the guise of ideologic principle. Social attitudes and political structures can thus legitimize what most would agree is morally unacceptable and destructive behavior. The antirape movement's philosophy in the late 1960s, which essentially grew out of the women's rights movement, is summarized by Largen[28]: "Rape is a universal problem for all women, not an individual problem for some... rape serves a social and political function in society by keeping women powerless" (p 4). Largen describes rape as something women have always had to contend with throughout history. And, among other authors, she cites Brownmiller[29] linking the act of rape "inextricably with war itself, as well as with race and class struggles"[28] (p 4). In regard to child sexual abuse, Rush[30] was the first feminist to place emphatically the blame of adult–child sex on the incestuous father or (usually male) child molester. She wrote that there is a long history of male sexual dominance over women and children. "One way or another," she asserted, "child molesters get permission for what they do. Adult-child sex is not a phenomenon that emerges from nowhere but is a legacy from the past which continues on in our everyday life" (p 15).

Changing social attitudes can also transform what was once regarded as morally corrupt behavior, for example, a premarital sexual relationship, into a more tolerated option. Recent movements such as feminist, sexual libertarian, and homosexual rights groups, advocating for individual sexual rights, have attempted to expand the range of what is considered normative in the current social climate. With regard to homosexuality, Bayer[31] writes that the social protest movements of the late 1960s served to encourage Gay Liberation groups to wage a campaign that in 1973 succeeded in making the Board of Trustees of the American Psychiatric Association to delete homosexuality from the sexual deviation category in their third edition of the *Diagnostic and Statistical Manual of Mental Disorders*.[32] Bayer qualifies this assertion, however, by noting that, while the Gay Liberation groups' protest played a significant role in this change, the ultimate success of the campaign depended as well on a combination of other contemporary factors, including the erosion of organized resistance on the part of the dissenting psychiatrists. Despite the fact that the official position of the American Psychiatric Association is no longer to regard homosexuality as a mental disorder, a comparable shift from the public's basically negative attitude toward homosexuality has not occurred. In fact, in his "Afterword" to the 1987 edition of his book, Bayer[31] expressed uncertainty about the direction of public response to homosexuality because of the increasing AIDS epidemic. Partly as a reaction to the liberal trends in the 1960s and 1970s, as well as to the upsurge of a "new moralism and the new right,"[33] (p 33) there has been a counter-conservative movement against and retrenchment within the so-called "sexual revolution." This has led to a more judgmental view in regard to sexual variation and deviant behavior in various quarters of society. This cross-current of contemporary sensibilities in recent years has made for a vociferous and lively social debate.

MODERN LEGAL-FORENSIC CONSIDERATIONS

The changing pattern in America's "sexual psychopath" statutes reflects not only basic ambiguities about coping with individuals who commit sexual crimes, but also the influences of societal pressures and prevailing philosophies and models of criminal justice. Special sexual psychopath laws, which were initially directed at the problem of sexual abuse of children, were enacted in Michigan in 1937. Subsequently, similar statutes were adopted in more than half of the other states by the mid-1960s. These laws had two basic goals: to remove offenders identified as having dangerous sexual propensities from the community, and to treat them.[34] A convicted sex offender was examined by psychiatrists and, if determined to be suffering from "sexual psychopathy" (legally defined in each state somewhat differently, but generally including a standard of mental illness and/or dangerousness), the offender was given an indeterminate sentence for medical treatment to last until he was no longer dangerous. This treatment approach was considered to be both scientific and humane, and it was consistent with the prevailing rehabilitative goals for offenders in general at the time.

According to Sutherland,[35] the development of sexual psychopath laws and their adoption by the various states generally occurred in three successive phases. First, a state of fear was produced in the community by the perpetration of several sensational sex crimes, particularly, sex murders of children. Second, an agitated community demanded action against sex crimes. Finally, a committee was appointed to ensure that appropriate action was taken. Frequently at this stage experts were called in to consult on the matter and to help in the formulation of public policy. Weisberg[36] has described how, at different periods in this century, legislators have used distinct types of experts—psychiatrists, psychologists, and social workers—to provide the major input on how society should respond to sexual abuse. In the 1930s, psychiatrists played the major role in labeling child molesters as people suffering from a mental condition termed "sexual psychopathy" requiring medical treatment. The first relabeling began in the 1950s as the sexual psychopath became the "mentally disordered sex offender," "sexual dangerous person," and "sexual deviate" in California, Illinois, and Wisconsin, respectively. This relabeling coincided with psychiatrists' disagreement about the basic nature of sexual abuse and about the legitimacy of the diagnosis of "sexual psychopathy," at a time when psychiatrists' frustration over the achievement of therapeutic goals was growing. Additionally, legal professionals were becoming increasingly critical of psychiatrists' role in the criminal justice system.[36] In 1977, the Group for the Advancement of Psychiatry (GAP) published *Psychiatry and Sex Psychopath Legislation: The 30s to the 80s*,[37] which stated: "We see special sex offender legislation as an approach to sex psychopaths that has failed, and consequently we feel these statutes should be repealed" (p 839). Emphasizing the confusing nature and lack of clinical validity of such terms as "sexual psychopathy" and "dangerousness," GAP argued that sex offenders are a heterogeneous group for which the "sexual psychopathy" label merely serves to stigmatize the individual and justify his removal from society. In the late 1960s and early 1970s, "psychologists and social workers gained increasing recognition by legislators as the preeminent experts in child sex crime issues."[36] The term "child molestation" started being replaced by either "sexual abuse" or "child sexual abuse" in new federal and state legislation. Intrafamilial child sexual abuse began to be viewed as not solely a perpetrator's problem, but as stemming at least in part from a dysfunctional system requiring family counseling. Treating the child victim became also a major priority.

By the 1980s, however, the pendulum had swung away from a rehabilitative approach toward criminal offenders to the current situation of competing ideologies in correctional treatment.[38] The justice model, with its emphasis on "just deserts" or "just punishments" and elimination of indeterminate sentencing, has in recent years been growing in popularity. Deviant sexual behavior, which had been first labeled by psychiatrists as "sexual psychopathy," and then relabeled by psychologists and social workers as "sexual abuse," was now increasingly being described as "sexual assault."[36] The continual discrediting of the clinical validity of "sexual psychopathy," combined with the push for abolition of sexual psychopath laws by many professional organizations,[34] has led increasing numbers of jurisdictions to repeal these statutes. By 1985, only 16 states and the District of Columbia still retained these laws, and only six of these states continued to actually enforce them.[39] Consequently, growing numbers of sex offenders are being sentenced under general penal regulations to determinate terms in prison rather than, as before, being processed by special dispositional alternatives to indeterminate sentences of psychiatric treatment.[40] The inadequacy of treatment opportunities in correctional facilities, however, was underscored by Borzecki and Wormith[41] in their survey of treatment programs for sex offenders in North America. These researchers found that only 21 out of the 31 states that provided information had any such program. The programs in the United States were generally located within correctional institutions, used the treatment modality of group psychotherapy with psychodynamic orientation, and lacked reliable outcome data. Not surprisingly, researchers concluded that these programs were unable to meet the treatment needs of the sex offenders.

CONCLUSION

Throughout modern history in the Western world, sexual perversions have been considered to be either immoral behaviors, or illegal behaviors, or both, worthy of either religious sanctions or legal punishments, particularly, if victims were involved. Although the medical establishment has in the past century and a half attempted to define sexually deviant behavior in psychiatric terms, society in general and the legal system in particular steadfastly perceive the problem also to be that of perverse criminal behavior. The complexity of the problem is that it is both a psychiatric disorder and a crime.[42] This reality presents the basic challenge to the sex therapist, who provides treatment to individuals suffering from a compulsive disorder which, if acted upon, constitutes a punishable crime. Ironically, the reduction of focus on rehabilitation and treatment in corrections is occurring at a time when more varied and effective treatment modalities are being introduced for sexual perversions. The focus of this book is basically on the theory and practice of these treatment modalities for sexual perversions. Before going into these treatment approaches, we will present some information on the extent of sexually deviant behavior in America.

REFERENCES

1. Bullough VL. *Sex, Society, and History.* New York, NY; Science History Publications; 1976.
2. Krafft-Ebing RV. *Psychopathia Sexualis.* Translated from the 12th German ed. New York, NY: Stein & Day Publishers; 1965.
3. Robinson P. *The Modernization of Sex.* Ithaca, NY: Cornell University Press; 1989.
4. Bullough VL *Sexual Variance in Society and History.* New York, NY: John Wiley & Sons; 1976.
5. Licht H. *Sexual Life in Ancient Greece.* New York, NY: Barnes & Nobles Inc; 1963.
6. Pike ER. *Love in Ancient Rome.* London, England: Frederick Muller Ltd; 1965.
7. Bullough VL. Historical perspective. *J Soc Work Hum Sexuality.* 1988; 7;15–23.
8. Cole WG. *Sex in Christianity and Psychoanalysis.* New York, NY: Oxford University Press; 1955.
9. Sussman N. Sex and sexuality in history. In: Sadock BJ, Kaplan HI, Freedman AM, eds. *The Sexual Experience.* Baltimore, Md: Williams & Wilkins; 1976; 7–70.
10. Kunitz SJ, Colby V, eds. *European Authors 1000–1900. A Biographical Dictionary of European Literature.* New York, NY: The HW Wilson Co; 1967.
11. *The Encyclopedia Britannica.* 15th ed. Chicago, Ill: Encyclopedia Britannica Inc; 1990.
12. Gonzalez-Crussi F. *On the Nature of Things Erotic.* San Diego, Calif: Harcourt Brace Jovanovich Publishers; 1988.
13. Brecher EM. *The Sex Researchers.* Boston, Mass: Little Brown & Co; 1969.

14. Blain D. Foreword, in *Psychopathia Sexualis*. Translated from the 12th German ed. New York, NY: Stein & Day Publishers; 1965.
15. Hirschfeld M. *Sexual Anomalies. The Origins, Nature, and Treatment of Sexual Disorders*. New York, NY: Emerson Books Inc, 1948,
16. Ellis H. *Studies in the Psychology of Sex, Vol I, II*. New York, NY: Random House; 1936.
17. Pomeroy WB. *Dr. Kinsey and the Institute for Sex Research*. New York, NY: Harper & Row; 1972.
18. Kinsey AC, Pomeroy WB, Martin CE. *Sexual Behavior in the Human Male*. Philadelphia, Pa: WB Saunders Co; 1948.
19. Kinsey AC, Pomeroy WB, Martin CE, Gebhard PH. *Sexual Behavior in the Human Female*. Philadelphia, Pa: WB Saunders Co; 1953.
20. Gebhard PH, Gagnon JH, Pomeroy WB, Christenson CV. *Sex Offenders: An Analysis of Types*. New York, NY: Harper & Row and Paul B Hoeber Inc Medical Books; 1965.
21. Freud S. Three Essays on the Theory of Sexuality. In: *Complete Psychological Works of Sigmund Freud*. Vol 7. London, England: Hogarth Press; 1905; 125–243.
22. Masters WH, Johnson VE. *Human Sexual Response*. Boston, Mass: Little Brown & Co; 1966.
23. Masters WH, Johnson VE. *Human Sexual Inadequacy*. Boston, Mass: Little Brown & Co; 1970.
24. Freund K. A laboratory method for diagnosing predominance of homo- and heteroerotic interest in the male. *Behav Res Ther*. 1963; 1:85–93.
25. Abel GG, Becker JV, Skinner LJ. Aggressive behavior and sex. In Meyer JK, ed. *Symposium on Sexuality. The Psychiatric Clinics of North America*. Vol 3, No. 1. Philadelphia, Pa: WB Saunders Company; April 1980.
26. Berlin FS, Meinecke CF. Treatment of sex offenders with antiandrogenic medication: conceptualization, review of treatment modalities, and preliminary findings. *Am J Psychiatry*. 1981;138:601–607.
27. Chasseguet-Smirgel J. *Creativity and Perversion*. New York, NY: WW Norton & Co; 1984.
28. Largen, MA. The anti-rape movement: past and present. In: Burgess AW, ed. *Rape and Sexual Assault. A Research Handbook*. New York, NY: Garland Publishing Inc; 1985.
29. Brownmiller S. *Against Our Will: Men, Women and Rape*. New York, NY: Simon & Schuster; 1975.
30. Rush F. *The Best Kept Secret: Sexual Abuse of Children*. New York, NY: McGraw-Hill International Book Co; 1980.
31. Bayer R. *Homosexuality and American Psychiatry. The Politics of Diagnosis*. Princeton, NJ: Princeton University Press; 1987.
32. *Diagnostic and Statistical Manual of Mental Disorders* (DMS-III). 3rd ed. Washington, DC: The American Psychiatric Association; 1980.
33. Weeks J. *Sexuality and Its Discontents. Meanings, Myths and Modern Sexualities*. London, England: Routledge & Kegan Paul; 1985.
34. Brakel SJ, Parry J, Weiner BA. Sexual Psychopath Laws. In: *The Mentally Disabled and the Law*. 3rd ed. Chicago, Ill: American Bar Foundation; 1985.
35. Sutherland EH. The diffusion of sexual psychopath laws. *Am J Sociol*. 1950;56:142–148.

36. Weisberg DK. The "discovery" of sexual abuse: experts' role in legal policy formulation. *UC Davis Law Rev.* 1984;18:1–57.
37. *Group for the Advancement of Psychiatry: Psychiatry and Sex Psychopath Legislation: The 30s to the 80s, Vol IX.* Publication No. 98. New York, NY: Mental Health Materials Center Inc; April 1977.
38. Bartollas C. *Correctional Treatment: Theory and Practice.* Englewood Cliffs, NJ: Prentice-Hall Inc; 1985.
39. Weiner BA. Legal issues raised in treating sex offenders. *Behav Sci Law.* 1985;3:325–340.
40. Dix GE. Special dispositional alternatives for abnormal offenders. Developments in the law. In: Monahan J, Steadman HJ, eds. *Mentally Disordered Offenders. Perspectives from Law and Social Science.* New York, NY: Plenum Press; 1983.
41. Borzecki M, Wormith JS. A survey of treatment programmes for sex offenders in North Ameria. *Can Psychol.* 1987;28:30–44.
42. Melella JT, Travin S, Cullen K. Legal and ethical issues in the use of antiandrogens in treating sex offenders. *Bull Am Acad Psychiatry Law.* 1989;17:223–232.

2

The Prevalence of Sexual Perversion

In all likelihood, the true prevalence rate of sexually perverse behavior will never be determined. Nonetheless, the studies now emerging are significantly increasing our understanding of the problem. Certainly, the more "benign" group of sexual perversions (for example, sadomasochistic fantasies experienced by patients who are seen in private practice) will probably never get reported and thus will never be included in statistical tabulations. Even the true extent of serious, sexually perverse acts that constitute sexual crimes perpetrated against victims, can only be estimated roughly, mainly because of gross underreporting and poor documentation. The lack of uniform definitions for such terms as sexual abuse and child molestation further exacerbates attempts to collect accurate data on prevalence.[1] Nevertheless, the urgent need to gain information about the true prevalence of sexually criminal behaviors has spurred efforts to collect such data. Despite the many shortcomings of the data available, estimates on prevalence are continually being extrapolated from sources of data that Finkelhor and Lewis[2] categorize into three main categories: criminologic, clinical, and survey orientations.

CRIMINOLOGIC DATA ON SEXUAL ASSAULTS

The major impetus sparking modern society's concern about sexually deviant behavior has been community perception of and concern about the prevalence of sex crimes. Periodically, evocative descriptions of sensational sex crimes capture public attention and outrage public consciousness. (It is worth noting, that even today Krafft-Ebing's[3] book on sex crimes, written nearly a century ago, makes spellbinding reading.) The transformation of public outrage about cases of child abuse, including sexual abuse, into society's perception of these abuses as social problems, is a subject of considerable importance. Nelson[4] has described how the revelations of extreme physical brutality in the Mary Ellen Wilson case were instrumental to the formation of the New York Society for the Prevention of Cruelty to Children in 1874. Following a subsequent period of declining interest in child abuse, the 1950s saw a reawakening of interest in the subject. This reawakening was caused in part by the burgeoning of concern that emerged during this period about a range of equal rights issues. But what really brought child abuse to the forefront of public attention, according to Nelson, were some startling case reports published in leading medical journals. In 1946, Caffey[5] published a number of cases about infants with multiple long bone fractures and subdural hematomas; after reexamining the data in 1957, Caffey concluded that the trauma could have been inflicted on these infants by their parents.[6] In 1962, Kempe et al[7] published their landmark article "The Battered-Child Syndrome" in the *Journal of the American Medical Association*. In this article, Kempe et al declared that the possibility of child abuse "should be considered in any child exhibiting evidence of fracture of any bone, subdural hematoma, failure to thrive, soft tissue swelling or skin bruising, [and] in any child who dies suddenly..."[7] (p 17).

Citing the history of public concern about and response to child abuse as a case in point, Nelson[4] explores the advantages and drawbacks encountered when social problems involving aggression and violence are explained in medical terms of deviance. He notes that such an explanation may be politically advantageous for two reasons: first, the particular behavior can be viewed

The Prevalence of Sexual Perversion

as a medical deviance from the statistical norm, and second, medicine usually offers solutions to the individual's illness. However, Nelson also points out the political limitations inherent in a medical deviance approach, including the negative impact on policymakers considering basic structural causes that require public funding, and the fact that individualized responses to social problems serve to perpetuate existing power relations, that may become contributing factors to the social problems. Nelson goes on to discuss how child abuse achieved governmental attention and response through agenda setting in the US Children's Bureau, mass and professional media, state legislatures, and congress. An important issue in itself, child abuse also proved to be an agenda-leading issue that paved the way for better governmental response to other problems such as rape, child sexual abuse, and child pornography.

The medicalization of sexual deviance with the enactment of sexual psychopath laws was an attempt to control sex crimes by scientific procedures rather than by punitive measures.[8] As we noted in the first chapter, Sutherland[8] has pointed out how these sexual psychopath laws were usually passed hastily in the state legislatures to alleviate community fear caused by sensational sex crimes, often crimes involving children; thus they constituted, among other things, a political response to a hysterical community demanding action, and were developed by a committee appointed by the state legislature for immediate performance. Among the sensational sex crimes Sutherland cites, that led to the creation of such laws, were the three or four sexual assaults (two of which culminated in murder) in Indianapolis in 1947, and the case of Fred Stroble, who was reported to have mutilated his victim in Los Angeles in 1949. Although most states have at some point been the scene of such crimes and the public outcry they ignite, not all states enacted sexual psychopath laws. In New York, for example, rather than enacting a sexual psychopath law in a panic following the murder of four girls in New York City, the mayor took certain emergency measures, but waited several months before appointing a committee to study the situation. This committee spent two years studying all sex crimes committed between 1930 and 1939 before reporting back to the mayor. As a result, New York State did not pass a sexual psychopath law.

In addition, to the different ways, then, in which states *define* "sex" crimes, attempts to ascertain the prevalence of such crimes are additionally confounded by some of the ways in which data is processed in the criminal justice system. These ways sometimes make it difficult to retrieve reliable data on the incidence of sex crimes.[9] A few examples amply illustrate such problems. The Specific Arrest Offense Crime Analysis Unit of the New York City Police Department reported the age range of offenders involved in 591 sex-related arrests in Bronx County in 1983, but not the age patterns of the victim. Incredibly, there were only two arrests per year for incest in the years 1981, 1982, and 1983 in Bronx County that has a population of approximately one million inhabitants. The two cases of incest per year recorded in the Bronx are consistent with the estimated 1.1 to 1.9 incest cases per million inhabitants reported in most criminal statistics in this country between 1910 and 1930.[10] While these examples illustrate the problems researchers confront in using data obtained from the criminal system, another and greater problem with criminologic data lies in the fact that in more than 90% of criminal cases, offenders plead to, and are ultimately convicted of, lesser charges. Gross underreporting of child sexual abuse appears to be even more of a problem than the underreporting of sex crimes committed against adults. Jaffe et al,[11] after a careful study of the police records in Minneapolis in 1970, found that one third of a total of 291 reported sex crimes were sexual crimes against children. In 11% of these reports, the sex crimes were rape, sodomy and/or sexual intercourse. Wells[12] estimated that 58% of a total of 2000 British rape victims were girls less than 13 years of age.

The American Association for Protecting Children (AAPC), the children's division of the American Humane Association in Denver, Colorado, has been compiling and analyzing national statistics on abuse and neglect since 1976.[13] Although only 28 states and territories provided the National Reporting Study with case level data, 2 086 000 children were reported as victims of child abuse and neglect to child protective services agencies in the United States and participating jurisdictions in 1986. Between

737 000 and 871 000 of these reports were substantiated. Sexual abuse cases represented 16% of all cases of maltreated children in 1986—a remarkable and disturbing increase from only 9% in 1983. Sexually abused children were predominantly female (77%), white (77%), and older (9.19 years); the perpetrators were predominantly male (82%), and a good number of them were either a parent (42%) or other relative (23%), and just over a third of them (35%) were unrelated to their victims. In a personal communication, Robyn Alsop, Information Services Coordinator at AAPC, reported that the estimated number of maltreated children reported to child protective services agencies in 1987 was 2 178 384, of which approximately 686 000 were confirmed by substantial data (this total figure has not yet been broken down into component categories of maltreatment). In addition, the task of compiling and analyzing national data on child abuse and neglect is now being continued by the US Department of Health and Human Services.

Responding to the need for reliable data on crimes against children, the New York State Division of Criminal Justice Services conducted a survey on the investigation and prosecution of crimes against children.[14] The study produced a number of findings about the problem of child victimization and the roles of the various law enforcement agencies in the state involved in the apprehension and prosecution of individuals committing crimes against children; this study concluded with recommendations for improving operational efficiency as well as for specialized law enforcement training. Among the total of 5911 arrests for crimes against children in New York State in 1986, 4161 or 70.4% were for "non-sexual offenses," 1620 or 27.4% for "sexual assaults," and 130 or 2.2% for "other sexual offenses." Of these "sexual assaults," 85.9% were at the felony level, including 710 arrests (40%) for such Class D felonies as rape 2, sodomy 2, or sexual abuse 1; and another 25% for such Class B felonies as rape 1 or sodomy 1.

As a follow-up to that report, the New York State Department of Correctional Services surveyed all new violent crime commitments to the Department in 1987 in order to determine what percentage of them involved child victims of physical or sexual offenses.[15] Among the 2026 males committed to the Department of Corrections for a physical or sexual offense, 462 (23%) of them had assaulted a child victim. The average age of these offenders was 35.4 years; most of them were white and from upstate New York. Seventy-seven percent of the child victims were female, and 23% were male. Female children were more likely to be sexually assaulted by a relative or by their mother's lover, while male children (23%) were more likely to be sexually assaulted by an acquaintance or a neighbor. On July 19, 1989, New York's Governor Cuomo established by executive order a Task Force to conduct a study on the crimes of rape and sexual assault. On January 9, 1990, the governor released the preliminary report that included recommendations that the state devise ways to combat stereotypes about victims of sexual assaults; develop adequate training requirements for those professionals working with victims and sex offenders; develop a policy regarding HIV/AIDS infection for victims; develop guidelines to ensure that sex offenses will be referenced, if plea-bargained to nonsex crimes; and develop new sex offender programs.[16]

Since 1930, the Federal Bureau of Investigation has been administering the Uniform Crime Reporting (UCR) Program, which receives and statistically analyzes data on reported crimes from approximately 16 000 law enforcement agencies throughout the country. Among the eight offenses that are collectively termed the "Crime Index" is the category of forcible rape against females. During 1988, an estimated 92 486 forcible rapes were reported which represented an increase of 2% over the preceding year. The 1988 estimate indicates that 73 out of every 100 000 females were reported to have been rape victims. In regard to persons arrested during 1988, law enforcement agencies reported 28 482 arrests for forcible rape and 78 239 for sex offenses (except forcible rape and prostitution), of which 72 522 were males and 5717 females.[17] A *New York Times* article of April 9, 1990 reported that the FBI recorded a still further increase of 1% in forcible rape during 1989.[18]

Another national measure of criminal victimization, the National Crime Survey (NCS), records crimes that are reported to the police as well as those that are not reported. The NCS records 1.3

rapes per 1000 females 12 years or older in 1987 and 1.2 in 1988. Forty-five percent of these rape victimizations were reported to the police.[19]

CLINICAL PERSPECTIVES ON PREVALENCE

Clinical contributions to appreciating the magnitude of the problem of sexual perversions have been made from the perspectives of victims and victimizers. A major obstacle in determining the true prevalence of sexual victimization, especially among children, has been the reluctance of parents and professionals alike to believe the victims' accusations. On April 27, 1984, the *New York Times* reported the testimony of Senator Paula Hawkins (R-Fla.) about her having been sexually abused by a middle-aged neighbor when she was a child of five, and how the judge did not believe her. Fortunately, Senator Hawkins' mother did believe the child, and was able to give her emotional support. Until very recently, even psychiatric clinicians have had difficulty believing reports by patients about childhood sexual victimization. Some critics argue that psychotherapists have tended to disbelieve patients' reports of childhood sexual abuse, and especially of seduction by their fathers, ever since Freud rejected his original seduction theory for etiology of hysteria in 1897. Afterward, Freud considered reports by patients of childhood seduction to be untrue and hysterical symptoms derived from fantasies.[20] In *The Best Kept Secret*,[21] Rush devotes an entire chapter to what she calls "a Freudian cover-up." Rush points out that in 1896 Freud had presented his seduction theory and substantiated it by citing a number of cases in which genital excitement resulting from sexual abuse in childhood had caused the patient's hysteria.[22] Drawing from the letters written by Freud to his close friend and confidant, Wilhelm Fliess,[23] a nose-and-throat specialist in Berlin, Rush[21] shows that Freud had actually named seduction by the father as the essential factor in the etiology of hysteria. However, outside of his correspondence to Fliess, Freud found it extremely difficult to go against the patriarchal society of the time and publicly name the father as seducer, even though many of his patients had reported this to him. Undergoing self-analysis during 1897, Freud confided to Fliess that he had growing suspicions about his own father and that he was concerned about a dream he had in which he felt overly affectionate toward his young daughter. Increasingly, Freud began to believe that the suspicions he felt about his own father and the stories of sexual seduction by fathers reported by patients were only memories of childhood fantasies, serving the need to experience the father as seducer. As Rush points out, by replacing the seduction theory with the Oedipus complex, Freud essentially shifted responsibility from father to daughter, and in doing so vindicated fathers as he implicated daughters.[21]

Just as the public (and psychiatric) proclivity to believe or disbelieve victims of sexual abuse has had enormous influence over perceptions of the prevalence of such crimes, so too has the question of psychiatric consequences of the trauma had considerable impact on public concerns about prevalence. Abraham,[24] an early disciple of Freud, believed that the child was unconsciously predisposed to engage in the incestuous activity and either initiated it or went along with it. Because the child probably felt guilty later on, she did not report it, but in any event, he argued, she did not subsequently develop a mental disorder. On the other hand, Ferenczi,[25] considered by many to be the greatest of Freud's disciples, in the last paper he published in 1933, emphasized the role of traumatic factors, and especially sexual trauma, in the pathogenesis of the neuroses. Ferenczi stressed that, more frequently than we suppose, parents or others responsible for the care of children misused this trust and sexually exploited them. Ferenczi argued that, because children feel physically and morally helpless in relationship to the authority figure, and because of their insufficiently developed personalities, their increased anxiety and fear cause them to subordinate themselves to the will of the aggressor, to gratify his desires, and to identify with the aggressor. This identification with the aggressor is accompanied by the "introjection of the guilt feelings of the adult . . . . " Later on the child "feels enormously confused, in fact, split—innocent and culpable at the same time—and his confidence in the testimony of his own senses is broken"[25] (p 202). Unfortunately, Ferenczi's views did not prevail: for decades, many writers tended to minimize the psychiatric sequelae of sexual victimization. For example, in 1937, Bender and Blau[26] wrote that the 16 preadolescent patients admitted to the Children's Ward of Bellevue Hospital in New York City following sexual activities with adults showed no signs of psychiatric disturbance. In a 1952 follow-up report of these 16 cases, Bender and Grugett[27] stated that early sexual activity did not necessarily result in maladaptive adjustments in adulthood. As recently as 1975, Henderson[28] asserted, in an influential psychiatric textbook, that daughters collude in, and even initiate, the incestuous liaison, and went on to assure his readers that these relationships "do not always seem to have a traumatic effect... the act offers an opportunity to test in reality an infantile fantasy whose consequences are found to be gratifying and pleasurable"[28] (p 1537).

With the exception of reports published by such an adult–child sex advocate organization as the North American Man/Boy Love Association (NAMBLA), the prevailing attitude among current writers is that sexual abuse directed against children and adults causes both proximate and long-term harmful psychological effects. In the case of child sexual abuse, the father or other adult is always considered the aggressor and the one solely responsible for the sexual activity. The child is always considered to be the victim and the one coerced into the sexual activity because of the pressure exerted on him or her by parental (or adult) authority.[29] The child is never considered to be competent to give informed consent for sex with an adult.[30]

Although most psychiatrists now perceive a causal relationship between child sexual abuse and emotional disturbance, the precise connection is often difficult to ascertain. In a study of 65 children and adolescents who had been psychiatrically hospitalized, of whom 37.5% of the nonpsychotic, 10% of the psychotic, and 8% of all the boys had a history of incest, Emslie and Rosenfeld[31] concluded that "social and psychological pathology serious enough to warrant hospitalization is not a simple effect of incest itself but is a consequence of severe family disorganization and the resulting ego impairment"[31] (p 708). On the other hand, Lewis and Sarrell[32] have described some "phase-specific" and "trauma-specific" manifestations of acute anxiety following seduction, incest, and rape. "Phase-specific" refers to the type of signs and symptoms found during a particular stage in the child's development, such as thumb-sucking, nail-biting, school difficulties, and delinquency; "trauma-specific" refers to the resemblance of the acting out behavior to reinforced fantasy material brought out by the sexual assault. Other researchers have found specific sequelae to child sexual abuse, including an increased frequency of severe psychological problems occurring in the 7- to 13-year-old group,[33] a correlation between the age at which and period of time over which children were molested by their fathers and the severity of the victims' psychological difficulties (children molested at an earlier age and/or over longer periods of time having more severe psychological problems than those molested at a later age and/or over a shorter period of time), severe psychological difficulties in teenagers even when they have been sexually victimized only once,[34] and a correlation between hysterical seizures in adolescents and a history of incest abuse.[35] Although the majority of these findings are based on studies of female victims, clinical cases of young males being sexually molested are increasingly being reported in the literature.[36,37] This is particularly significant because, although both male and female children who are victims of sexual abuse experience a post-sexual-abuse syndrome similar to that of the adult rape victim, the male victim is more likely to externalize his rage into aggressive and antisocial behavior.[38]

Clinical reports of adults suffering from the sequelae of child sexual victimization and undergoing psychiatric treatment in a variety of settings form a sizable part of the current literature in mental health. Katan[39] has written about two female patients she psychoanalyzed, one for constant agitation, anxieties, and depression, and the other for severe depression and a paralyzing fear of men. Both women had been sexually victimized as small children, the first by her father and the second by the nursemaid's boyfriend. Katan found that, of the six women she treated who had similar histories of child sexual victimization, all six tended to repeat the traumatic incidents in various ways; some failed to prevent the sexual victimizations of their own children in a kind of repetition compulsion; and all suffered from extremely low self-esteem. Briere et al[40] examined the long-term sequelae of 40 male and 40 female clients with histories of childhood sexual victimization, who were seen in the crisis counseling program of a community health center. The authors concluded that with reference to symptomatology there was no difference between the male and female sexual abuse victims. In an earlier study, Sarrell and Masters[41] had reported on 11 cases of males who had been sexually abused (at different ages) by females; all 11 men, they found, suffered a post-trauma reaction comparable to the rape-trauma syndrome experienced by adult female rape victims. In regard to the prevalence and possible relevance of childhood sexual victimization among psychiatric inpatients, Jacobson and Herald[42] found that 40 out of 100 inpatients reported some form of abuse, and 18 of them reported major abuse. Interestingly, there were no gender differences among the major abuse cases. The authors conclude that inquiring about childhood sexual abuse is justified in order to make the correct diagnosis and treatment plans. Through an in-depth examination of psychiatric inpatient records, Carmen et al[43] found that almost half of 188 male and female adult patients had histories of physical and/or sexual victimization. The abused males were more likely to have been violent to others, while the females more frequently had directed their anger and violence against themselves.

The growing consensus among clinicians, evident in the research we have been discussing, that sexual assaults cause severe negative consequences to victims, clearly applies to the subject of rape. Although the antirape movement of the early 1970s stimulated the creation of such self-help programs as rape crisis center that provided emergency crisis intervention services, Largen[44] points out that Burgess and Holmstrom's publication in 1974 of *Rape: Victims of Crisis*[45] helped to validate the centers' theories and practices. This book also contributed to the legitimization of further medical and mental health professionals' involvement in providing victim services. With their numerous publications on rape, including an early description of the rape trauma syndrome,[46] and with the subsequent incorporation of this syndrome in the category of post-traumatic stress disorder[47] in the third edition of the American Psychiatric Association's *Diagnostic and Statistical Manual*,[48] Burgess and Holmstrom have made at least two significant contributions: they have clarified the status of the raped as victims and increased our understanding of approaches to the treatment of rape victims. Increasingly, hospital emergency services have been developing and implementing their own rape and sexual assault protocols to provide for the treatment of such victims. Such trends are leading to not only more humane and effective treatment for rape victims, but also to a new source of data on the prevalence and specifications of sexual assaults, for some hospitals' rape and sexual assault protocols, in addition to addressing the provision of emergency life-saving procedures, medical treatment, crisis intervention counseling, and referral, also initiate the documentation and collection of specimens for forensic purposes.

Although the clinical perspective including assessment and treatment issues on those sexually perverse individuals who victimize others will be discussed in detail later on, some points about their use of force and the number of their victims should be made here. In their 1981 study of sex offenders coming for evaluation and treatment in their outpatient program, Abel et al[49] found that these offenders, now outpatients who were assured of the confidentiality of their reports, admitted to an average number of assaults per offender by primary diagnostic classification as follows: heterosexual incest—2.1; heterosexual rape—5.8; homosexual pedophilia—30.6; heterosexual pedophilia—62.4; exhibitionism—199.5; and frottage (which usually involves rubbing one's genitals against a victim in a crowded place such as a public transportation vehicle)—582.8. These data simultaneously reveal the tremendous numbers of victims of sexual offenders and the gross underreporting of such assaults in police records. Abel et al[49] also cite Christie, Marshall, and Lanthier's 1978 report to the Solicitor General of Canada[50] on the findings in their study of 150 incarcerated sex offenders, of which 27% were pedophiles and 73% heterosexual rapists. These researchers found that "58% of the child molesters used excessive physical force during the crime, compared to 71% of the rapists. Moreover, 42% of the child victims sustained noticeable injury, compared to 39% of the rape victims"[49] (p 119). Christie et al[50] concluded that contrary to earlier reports that depicted pedophiles as being physically harmless to their victims, the data of their group revealed that a substantial number of these pedophiles used excessive force during the crime, and that this revelation constituted sufficient evidence to justify and even urge further research into the matter.[49]

Another clinical point about victimizers concerns the incidence of sexual abuse committed by females compared with the incidence perpetrated by males. In a review of convictions for sexual offenses from 1975 to 1984 in England and Wales, O'Connor[51] found that 0.95% of the total number were committed by females. Similarly, Groth and Birnbaum[52] had found that approximately 1% (3 out of 253) of incarcerated child molesters were female. Travin et al[53] have reported that only five females (1% of a total of 515 sexual offenders) had been referred to their specialized sex-offender treatment program, although they treated an additional four females who had committed acts of sexual abuse but had not been apprehended for these crimes by any law enforcement agency. Similarly, in their 1987 study of 44 identified treatment agencies throughout the country, Knopp and Lackey[54] noted that 40 of these agencies had reported that they were treating a total of 256 female sexual abusers.

Although most researchers agree that the incidence rate of female sexual abusers is considerably less than that of male sexual abusers, estimates of the true incidence rate are rough at best, as data on female sexual abusers is suspected to be undermined by not only underreporting, but also because of several other factors, including the disguising of female sexual acts with children as normal maternal care, the reluctance of children dependent on their mothers to report incestuous activities, and the frequent misinterpretation by young boys of the abusive nature of these sexual incidents because of social conditioning.[53]

SURVEY DATA ON SEXUAL ABUSE

In recent years, our increasing realization of the inadequacy of available data and of the need for more accurate knowledge of sexual abuse, has led researchers more and more to conduct surveys of diverse populations on sexual assault outside of the criminologic and clinical areas in order to obtain more representative samples and to compensate for many cases that are not detected or reported.[2] Though the emphasis has been mostly on surveys of victims rather than of offenders, researchers are now beginning to study undetected offenders. While researchers are continually refining their survey methodologies in order to gain a better understanding of the nature and scope of sexual abuse, even the earlier surveys, in spite of their notable shortcomings, have added significantly to our knowledge of the problem.

Although Kinsey is credited with the largest and most extraordinary surveys still extant, he is also criticized for failing to appreciate the significance of sexual child abuse. In their study of male sexuality, Kinsey et al[55] reported that "only a few males have intercourse with very young girls," and that "homosexual incest occurs more frequently in the thinking of clinicians and social workers than it does in actual performance"; they went on to assert that "the most frequent incestuous contacts are between preadolescent children, but the number of such cases among adolescent or older males is very small"[55] (p 558). Russell[56] questions why Kinsey did not provide any data about incest among preadolescent children, and refers to Herman's[57] suggestion that the Kinsey researchers seemed to be concerned less about the personal integrity of the child than about the "sensitivity" of men who might be accused of sexual assault by children or women. Yet in their nonrandom survey of 4441 white middle-class females who were interviewed and questioned about childhood sexual encounters, Kinsey et al[58] found that 1075 of these women— 24%— reported having been approached in a sexual manner by adult males while they were still preadolescents. The majority of those sexual contacts involved males exhibiting their genitalia followed by instances of fondling without genital contact, with approximately 3% culminating in actual coitus. The researchers commented that in 80% of these cases the sexual encounter was a lone experience. However, in those instances where there were repeated sexual encounters, they occurred with relatives residing in the same household, and the researchers attributed the fault to the children: "In many instances the experiences were repeated because the children had become interested in the sexual activity and had more or less actively sought repetitions of that experience"[58] (p 118).

Although the Kinsey researchers acknowledged that some 80% of the children had experienced negative reactions to sexual encounters with adults, they believed the reactions were no more serious than a child's reactions when shown a spider or other adversely conditional object. "It's difficult to understand why a child, except for its cultural conditioning, should be disturbed at having its genitalia touched," they opined, "or disturbed at seeing the genitalia of other persons, or disturbed at even more specific sexual contacts"[58] (p 121). By this minimalization of the consequences of sexual abuse, and by their explicitly ignoring and implicitly denying the child's powerlessness, Russell[56] believes that the Kinsey researchers reveal at least a tolerance of, and possibly their own positive bias toward, incest. Herman had earlier concluded that these researchers, in "ignoring issues of dominance and power... took a license that amounted to little more than advocacy of greater sexual license for men"[57] (p 17).

The problematic nature of Kinsey's survey is emphasized by the fact that contemporary researchers working with Kinsey's study arrive at contradictory numbers of cases to be used in the statistical analysis. Extrapolating from Kinsey's data, Herman[57] estimated that these researchers had interviewed the largest number of women in the general population who reported having had preadolescent incestuous relations, 40 of them with their fathers and an additional 300 with older male relatives. In comparison, Russell,[56] using the same Kinsey data, but calculating from a different total of case samples (609 versus 1039)[58] estimated that there were 24 cases of father–daughter incest and 115 cases of other incestuous abuse, representing an approximate 3% prevalence rate of preadolescent incest—a rate considerably less than the 12% prevalence rate of preadolescent incestuous abuse Russell found in her study of incest. Indeed, Russell believes incestuous abuse before the age of 18 and extrafamilial child sexual abuse before the age of 14, have significantly increased between early 1900 and 1973 owing to a combination of factors such as the sexualization of children and child pornography; the so-called sexual revolution with its more accepting attitude; the backlash against sexual equality created by increasing numbers of men terrified of dealing with adult women as equals; the significant number of perpetrators who were themselves untreated victims of child sexual abuse; and the greatly increased incidence of stepfamilies in American society (in Russell's probability sample, 17% of the women had been sexually involved with stepfathers).

In their book, *The Sexual Abuse of Children*, Haugaard and Reppucci[59] have summarized the results of different surveys and discussed some of the methodological limitations in these studies. In general, two factors that limit research efficacy are the rate of participation of possible subjects in the sample group, and the honest participation of these subjects. The limiting factors of large-scale surveys then involve the choice of a particular group to be surveyed as representative of a larger group and the elicitation of maximum and honest participation from this group. The advantage of surveying a special sample lies in the efficiency with which a concentrated number of sexual abuse victims can be studied, and in avoiding the need to survey many people. However, the issue of honesty may become an even greater concern in special samples; for example, sex offenders may tend to overreport their own victimization in order to justify their sexual assaults on others. Clearly, each type of sample carries certain limitations and poses particular challenges to researchers. Haugaard and Reppucci stress the limitations specific to each type of sample, and suggest that only by utilizing a wide range of samples can we reduce the margin of error in research on prevalence.

A few samples of the many large-scale surveys Haugaard and Reppucci cite and summarize suggest the variety and range of these surveys, as well as the discrepancies and difficulties in their findings. The national samples of Kinsey et al,[58] as we have noticed, stated that 24% of the interviewed women reported having had a childhood sexual experience with an adult male; similarly, the Canadian Government Population Survey of 1984[60] found that 28% of the women and 10% of the men had experience some sort of childhood sexual abuse. The samples of urban women included Russell's[61] finding that 28% of the 930 women interviewed reported some form of sexual abuse involving contact before their 14th birthday, and 38% reported such abuse before their 18th birthday. If noncontact sexual abuse (such as being victimized by an adult exhibitionist) is also considered, then 54%

of the women had been abused before their 18th birthday. The college surveys included Landis'[62] 1956 survey of 1800 college students which, using an anonymous questionnaire found that 35% of the females and 30% of the men reported having been sexually abused as children, while Finkelhor's[63] survey of 796 undergraduates in six New England colleges found that 19% of the women and 9% of the men had been sexually victimized as children.

Among the surveys of special populations described by the authors, the following merit particular mention: James and Meyerdings'[64] 1977 study of 136 prostitutes, which found that 52% had experienced some form of child sexual abuse; McCormack, James, and Burgess'[65] 1986 study of 149 runaway children in a shelter in Toronto that revealed that 73% of the females and 38% of the males had been sexually victimized; Jones, Gruber, and Timber's[66] 1981 report on the results of interviewing 66 adolescents involved with residential delinquency-treatment programs in the Appalachia region, which found that, of the 42 female adolescents interviewed, 33% had been raped and an additional 16% had been sexually assaulted. In 19% of these cases the assaults had been perpetrated by stepfathers or foster fathers.

Interestingly, there are differing opinions as to the extent of stepfathers sexual abuse of their children compared with that of biological fathers. In her sample of 930 interviews with adult women, Russell[67] found that 17%, or one of six, of the women who had stepfathers had been molested by them, and in 47% of the cases the molestation comprised either fellatio or sexual intercourse, compared to the 2% of women who were sexually abused by their natural fathers, which involved only 2% at the very serious level. In contrast, Phelan[68] who interviewed the data on 56 incestuous stepfather families and 46 incestuous biological father families, found that biological fathers sexually abused their daughters more frequently and seriously, including sexual intercourse, than did stepfathers.

Concerning the epidemiologic approach to gaining information about undetected offenders, Finkelhor and Lewis[2] point out that more progress has been made with rapists and rape-prone individuals[69,70] than with child molesters. Obviously, a large number of child molesters go undetected; this can be deduced from the high prevalence rates on victimization. In an attempt to identify undetected child molesters, Finkelhor and Lewis[2] employed a variation of a highly experimental technique called Randomized Response Technique,[71] which consists in pairing a sensitive question with an innocuous one presented simultaneously to the subject. In a telephone survey of 2627 adults, the researchers found that in one sample of paired questions, 17% of the respondents answered "yes" to whether they had ever sexually abused a child, and in a second sample of paired questions 4% did. Despite the experimental nature of the technique and the discussion of which of the two sets of paired questions produces word-accurate results, the fact is that "the mean of the two estimates in the current survey, 10%, is on the high side but within the realm of plausibility"[2] (p 70). Because of the widespread nature of this behavior, Finkelhor and Lewis argue that sociopsychological concepts, including aspects of masculine socialization, such as the need for dominance, will have to be considered if we are to understand how they contribute to the problem of sexual abuse.

CONCLUSION

As the cumulative data indicate, sexually perverse behavior is common. Indeed, sexually deviant behaviors, ranging from the "benign" to serious sexual crimes, are so common that now as in the past one is hard-pressed to believe the findings of these reports on frequency of occurrence. Our individual reactions to emerging data on the prevalence rates of sexually deviant behaviors should not surprise us; after all, even such giants as Freud and Kinsey, both of whom regarded themselves as being objective scientists, could not dispassionately appraise the significance of their own findings. Evidently, the subject of sexuality, particularly, of perverse sexuality, taps into a variety of deep emotions in most of us.

Nonetheless, the net impact of receiving, in so many different ways, the information on the prevalence of sexually perverse behaviors, is to help overcome our natural reluctance to face the reality of such common human behaviors, indeed, the reality that such behaviors *are* human and *are* common. The importance of ascertaining and publicizing more accurate prevalence rates of sexually perverse behaviors cannot, then, be overrated, for it is only by gaining an appreciation of the true extent of these behaviors that we will make the effort to understand and to do something about them.

REFERENCES

1. Barnard GW, Fuller AK, Robbins L, Shaw T. *The Child Molester: An Integrated Approach to Evaluation and Treatment*. San Francisco, Calif: Jossey-Bass Publishers; 1989.
2. Finkelhor D, Lewis IA. An epidemiologic approach to the study of child molestation. In: Prentky RA, Quinsey VL, eds. *Human Sexual Aggression: Current Perspectives*. Annals of the New York Academy of Sciences. Vol 528. New York, NY: The New York Academy of Sciences; 1988.
3. Krafft-Ebing RV. *Psychopathia Sexualis*. Translated from the 12th German ed. New York, NY: Stein & Day Publishers; 1965.
4. Nelson BJ. *Making an Issue of Child Abuse. Political Agenda Setting for Social Problems*. Chicago, Ill: The University of Chicago Press; 1984.
5. Caffey J. Multiple fractures in the long bones of infants suffering from chronic subdural hematoma. *AJR*. 1946; 56:163–173.
6. Caffey J: Some traumatic lesions in growing bones other than fractures and dislocation—clinical and radiological features. *Br J Radiol*. 1957;30:225–238.
7. Kempe CH, Silverman FN, Steel BF, Droegemueller W, Silver HK. The Battered Child Syndrome. *JAMA*. 1962;181:17–24.
8. Sutherland EH. The diffusion of sexual psychopath laws. *Am J Sociol*. 1950;56: 142–148.
9. Travin S, Bluestone H, Coleman E, Cullen L, Melella J. Pedophilia: an update on theory and practice. *Psychiatr Q*. 1985; 57:89–103.
10. Weinberg SK. *Incest Behavior*. New York, NY: Citadel Press; 1955.
11. Jaffe AC, Dynneson L, Bensel HWT. Sexual abuse of children: an epidemiologic study. *AJDC*. 1975;129:689–692.
12. Wells NH. Sexual offenses as seen by a woman police surgeon. *Br Med J*. 1958;5109:1404–1408.
13. *Highlights of Official Child Neglect and Abuse Reporting 1986*. Denver, Colo: The American Humane Association; 1988.
14. New York State Division of Criminal Justice Services. The Investigation and Prosecution of Crimes Against Children in New York State. Albany, NY: April 1988.
15. *New York State Department of Correctional Services. Commitments Involving Child Victims of Physical or Sexual Offenses*. Albany, NY: December 1988.
16. *Governor's Task Force on Rape and Sexual Assault: Preliminary Recommendations*. Albany, NY: November 1989.

17. *Uniform Crime Reports for the United States. U.S. Department of Justice. Federal Bureau of Investigation.* Washington, DC: US Government Printing Office; August 6, 1989.
18. *The New York Times. Crimes of Violence are up 5% in U.S.* Monday, April 9, 1990.
19. Bureau of Justice Statistics Bulletin. *Criminal Victimization 1988.* Washington, DC: US Department of Justice; October 1989.
20. Freud S. *The Complete Introductory Lectures of Psychoanalysis.* New York, NY: Norton; 1966.
21. Rush F. *The best kept secret: sexual abuse of children.* Englewood Cliffs, NJ: Prentice-Hall Inc; 1980.
22. Freud, S, Strackey J, trans. Studies on Hysteria. In: *The Standard Edition of the Complete Psychological Works.* Vol II. London, England: The Hogarth Press; 1955.
23. Freud S; Bonaparte M, Freud A, Kris E, eds. Mosbacher, E., J. Strachey, trans. *The Origins of Psychoanalysis, letters to Wilhelm Fliees. Drafts and Notes: 1887–1902.* New York, NY: Basic Books; 1954.
24. Abraham K. The experiencing of sexual traumas as a form of sexual activity. In: *Selected Papers of Karl Abraham.* London, England: Hogarth Press; 1927.
25. Ferenczi S. Confusion of tongues between adults and the child. *Contemp Psychoanal.* 1988;24:196–206.
26. Bender L, Blau A. The reaction of children to sexual relations with adults. *Am J Orthopsychiatry.* 1937;7:500–518.
27. Bender L, Grugett FAE. A follow-up report on children who had atypical sexual experiences. *Am J Orthopsychiatry.* 1952;22:825–837.
28. Henderson D; Incest. In: Freedman AM, Kaplan HI, Sadock BJ eds. *Comprehensive Textbook of Psychiatry.* Vol 2, 2nd ed. Baltimore, Md: Williams & Wilkins; 1975.
29. Burgess AW, Holmstrom LL. Sexual trauma of children and adolescents: pressure, sex, and secrecy. *Nurs Clin North Am* 1975;10:551–563.
30. Abel GG, Becker JV, Cunningham-Rathner J. Complications, consent and cognitions in sex between children and adults. *Int J Law Psychiatry.* 1984;7:89–103.
31. Emslie GJ, Rosenfeld A. Incest reported by children and adolescents hospitalized for severe psychiatric problems. *Am J Psychiatry.* 1983;140:708–711.
32. Lewis M, Sarrell PM. Some psychological aspects of seduction, incest and rape. *J Am Acad Child Psychiatry.* 1969;8:606–619.
33. Gomes-Schwartz B, Horowitz M, Sauzier M. Severity of emotional distress among sexually abused preschool, school-age, and adolescent children. *Hosp Comm Psychaitry.* 1985;36:503–508.
34. Adams-Tucker C. Proximate effects of sexual abuse in childhood: a report on 28 children. *Am J Psychiatry.* 1982;139:1252–1256.
35. Gross M. Incestuous rape: a cause for hysterical seizures in four adolescent girls. *Am J Orthopsychiatry.* 1979;49:704–708.
36. Dixon KN, Arnold LE, Calestrok. Father-son incest: underreported psychiatric problem? *Am J Psychiatry.* 1978;135:835–838.
37. Johnson RL, Shrier D. Past sexual victimization by females of male patients in an adolescent medicine clinic population. *Am J Psychiatry.* 1987;144:650–652.
38. Summit RC. The child sexual abuse accommodation syndrome. *Child Abuse Neglect.* 1983;7:177–193.
39. Katan A. Children who were raped. *Psychoanal Study Child.* 1973;28:208–224.
40. Briere J, Evans D, Runtz M, Wall T. Symptomatology in men who were molested as children: a comparison study. *Am J Orthopsychiatry.* 1988;58:457–461.

41. Sarrell PM, Masters WH. Sexual molestation of men by women. *Archives of Sexual Behavior.* 1982;11:117–131.
42. Jacobson A, Herald C. The relevance of childhood sexual abuse to adult psychiatric inpatient care. *Hosp Comm Psychiatry.* 1990;41:154–158.
43. Carmen EH, Rieker PP, Mills T. Victims of violence and psychiatric illness. *Am J Psychiatry.* 1984;141:378–383.
44. Largen MA. The anti-rape movement past and present. In: Burgess AW ed. *Rape and Sexual Assault. A Research Handbook.* New York, NY: Garland Publishing Inc; 1985.
45. Burgess AW, Holmstrom LL. *Rape: Victim of Crisis.* Bowie, Md: Brady Company; 1974.
46. Burgess AW, Holmstrom LL. Rape trauma syndrome. *Am J Psychiatry.* 1974; 131:981–986.
47. Burgess AW, Holmstrom LL. Rape trauma syndrome and post traumatic stress response. In: Burgess AW, ed. *Rape and Sexual Assault. A Research Handbook.* New York, NY: Garland Publishing Inc; 1985.
48. American Psychiatric Association. *Diagnostic and Statistical Manual of Mental Disorders (DSM-III).* 3rd ed, Washington, DC: American Psychiatric Association; 1980.
49. Abel GG, Becker JV, Murphy WE, Flanagan B. Identifying dangerous child molesters. In: Stuart R, ed. *Violent Behavior—Social Learning Approaches to Prediction. Management and Treatment.* New York, NY: Brunner/Mazel; 1981.
50. Christie M, Marshall W, Lanthier R. *A Descriptive Study of Incarcerated Rapists and Pedophiles.* Report to the Solicitor General of Canada. Ottawa, Canada: 1979.
51. O'Connor AA. Female sex offenders. *Br J Psychiatry.* 1987;150:515–520.
52. Groth AN, Birnbaum HJ. *Men Who Rape: The Psychology of the Offenders.* New York, NY: Plenum Press; 1979.
53. Travin S, Cullen K, Protter B. Female sex offender: Severe victims and victimizers. *J Forensic Sci.* 1990;35:140–150.
54. Knopp FH, Lackey LB. *Female Sexual Abusers: A Summary of Data from 44 Treatment Providers.* The Safer Society Program of the New York State Council of Churches. Orwell, Vt, October 1987.
55. Kinsey AC, Pomeroy WB, Martin CE. *Sexual Behavior in the Human Male.* Philadelphia, Pa: WB Saunders Co; 1948.
56. Russell DEH: *The Secret Trauma. Incest in the lives of girls and women.* New York, NY: Basic Books Inc; 1986.
57. Herman JL. *Father-Daughter Incest.* Cambridge, Mass: Harvard University Press; 1981.
58. Kinsey AC, Pomeroy WB, Martin CE, Gebhard PH. *Sexual Behavior in the Human Female.* Philadelphia, Pa: WB Saunders Co; 1953.
59. Haugaard JJ, Reppucci ND. *The Sexual Abuse of Children.* San Francisco, Calif: Jossey-Bass Publisher; 1988.
60. Committee on Sexual Offenses Against Children and Youth. *Sexual Offenses Against Children.* Ottawa, Canada: Canadian Publishing Center; 1984.
61. Russell DEH. The incidence and prevalence of intrafamilial and extrafamilial sexual abuse of female children. *Child Abuse Neglect.* 1983;7:133–146.
62. Landis JT. Experiences of 500 children with adult sexual deviants. *Psychiatr Q* (suppl) 1956;30:91–109.
63. Finkelhor D. *Sexually Victimized Children.* New York, NY: Free Press; 1979.

64. James J, Meyerding J. Early sexual experience as a factor in prostitution. *Arch Sex Behav.* 1978;7:31–42.
65. McCormack A, James MD, Burgess AW. Runaway youths and sexual victimization: gender differences in an adolescent runaway population. *Child Abuse Neglect.* 1986;10:387–395.
66. Jones RJ, Gruber KJ, Timbers GD. Incidence and situational factors surrounding sexual assault against delinquent youth. *Child Abuse Neglect.* 1981;5:431–440.
67. Russell DEH. The prevalence and seriousness of incestuous abuse: stepfathers vs. biological fathers. *Child Abuse Neglect.* 1984;8:15–22.
68. Phelan P. The process of incest: biologic father and stepfather families. *Child Abuse Neglect.* 1986;10:531–539.
69. Kanin EJ. Date rapists: differential sexual socialization and relative deprivation. *Arch Sex Behav.* 1985;14:219–231.
70. Malamuth NM. Rape proclivity among males. *Soc Issues.* 1981;37:138–157.
71. Folsom RE, Greenberg BG, Horvitz DG, Abernathy JR. The two alternative questions randomized response model for human surveys. *J Am Stat Assoc.* 1973;68:525–530.

3

The Diagnosis and Classification of Sexual Perversion

The diagnosis and classification of sexually deviant disorders, like the diagnosis and classification of mental disorders in general, are continually evolving, for they reflect the way sexually deviant disorders are perceived.[1] Classificatory systems incorporate current perceptions of mental disorders into categories whose purposes are, according to Spitzer and Williams,[2] to promote "communication, control, and comprehension" (p 591). Communication depends on using the names of categories to stand for previously agreed on criteria meriting inclusion into these categories. Control implies being able to prevent mental disorders from occurring, or having sufficient knowledge about their natural courses to modify them. Comprehension means having sufficient understanding about the causes, developments, and treatments of these disorders to control or cure them.

The first official compilation of mental disorders in the United States began in the decennial census of 1840 in which the sole category of mental disorders included both the idiotic and the insane. Since then a succession of systems for classifying mental disorders has been used. In 1952, the American Psychiatric Association published the first edition of the *Diagnostic and Statistical Manual of Mental Disorders* (DSM-I),[3] which presented a glossary of definitions of diagnostic categories. This work provides a good example of the ways in which contemporary perceptions of sexually deviant disorders shape the diagnosis and classification of these disorders. The frequent appearance of the term "reaction" in this first edition of the DSM, for example, points to an environmental orientation, while the frequent mention of defense mechanisms for explanatory purposes reflects psychoanalytic influence. The second edition of this work, the DSM-II,[4] published in 1965, for the most part dropped the term "reaction."[2] And, as Klerman[5] points out, the third edition, published in 1980, with its assimilation of clinical experience and research advances, and its reaffirmation of the concept of multiple separate disorders, clearly "placed psychiatry once again within the classic model that arose in the eighteenth and nineteenth centuries" (p 70). Klerman identifies some of the innovations of the DSM-III as follows: the first official nomenclature to use inclusive and exclusionary criteria that are largely based on manifest descriptive psychopathology rather than on speculation as to causation; a multiaxial system; and a nomenclature tested in the field for reliability.

Spitzer and Williams[2] acknowledge that the "criteria-based categorical typologies" (p 619) improve diagnostic reliability, but they question whether or not the typologies "reflect the 'real world' experience of the practitioner" (p 619). Spitzer and Williams are concerned that the categorical typologies of the DSM-III[6] are for the most part "normative" (ie, based on expert opinion) rather than "empirical" (ie, based on statistical analysis). Even if normative typologies achieve high interrater reliability, Spitzer and Williams suggest that normative-based typologies may be "as idiosyncratic as the more inferential clinical processes that they are attempting to improve upon" (p 619). These comments on normative typologies have particular relevance to the construction of diagnostic categories for paraphiliac disorders because of the scarcity of statistical data and the consequent reliance on expert opinion in this area.

PSYCHIATRIC DIAGNOSES OF SEXUAL PERVERSIONS

The diverse ways in which such terms as "child molester" and "dangerousness" have been defined over the past 40 years[7] highlight the need for standardized diagnostic criteria for sexually deviant behaviors. This diversity can be traced in the American Psychiatric Association's four successive editions of the *Diagnostic and Statistical Manual of Mental Disorders*, each of which has updated the operational categorizations of sexual deviations. In the DSM-I, "Sexual Deviations" were listed along with "Antisocial Reaction" and "Dyssocial Reaction" under the heading "Sociopathic Personality Disturbance," which was itself subsumed under the overall category of "Personality Disorders." There were no subdivisions listed under the "Sexual Deviation" heading. This categorization of sexual deviation reflected the prevailing notion that the sexually deviant individual was "ill primarily in terms of lack of conformity with society and prevailing cultural milieu, not just in terms of individual relationships and personal discomfort"[8] (p 1066). In the DSM-II, "Sexual Deviations" were listed as a separate division with nine subdivisions, including homosexuality, fetishism, and pedophilia. But "Sexual Deviations," along with "Personality Disorders," "Alcoholism," and "Drug Dependence" were still grouped under the overall category V of "Personality Disorders and Certain Other Non-Psychotic Mental Disorders." The "Sexual Deviations" category was meant for individuals "whose sexual interests are directed primarily toward objects other than people of the opposite sex, toward sexual acts not usually associated with coitus, or toward coitus performed under bizarre circumstances..." (p 44).

In the DSM-III,[6] "Sexual Deviations" were replaced by the term "Paraphilia," which, as the DSM-III asserted, "correctly emphasizes that the deviation (para) is in that to which the individual is attracted (philia)" (p 267). "Paraphilia" was included in the general category of "Psychosexual Disorders" without any regard to personality disorder concerns. Also included under Psychosexual Disorders were "Gender Identity Disorders," "Psychosexual Dysfunctions," and "Other Psychosexual Disorders," this last category enveloping "Ego-dystonic Homosexuality" and "Psychosexual Disorders Not Elsewhere Classified." The DSM-III thus identified the essential features of paraphiliac behaviors as their repeated, preferred, and exclusive demands. In keeping with this emphasis, the diagnostic criteria for zoophilia, to take one example of paraphiliac behavior, described zoophilia as "the act or fantasy of engaging in sexual activity with animals as a repeatedly preferred or exclusive method of achieving sexual excitement" (p 270). Thus, paraphilia was inconsistently defined as requiring either deviant acts, or merely deviant fantasies.

This inconsistency was overcome in the DSM-III-R, the revised version of the DSM-III published by the American Psychiatric Association in 1987. The DSM-III-R contains a consistent set of diagnostic criteria for all paraphilias, adding the dimension of duration and underscoring the intensity of the urges and fantasies. The severity of the manifestations is delineated as follows: "Mild: The person is markedly distressed by the recurrent paraphiliac urges, but never acted on them. Moderate: the person has occasionally acted on the paraphiliac urge. Severe: The person has repeatedly acted on the paraphiliac urge" (p 281). In keeping with this emphasis on duration and intensity, the diagnostic criteria for pedophilia in the DSM-III-R reads as follows: "Over a period of at least six months, recurrent intense sexual urges and sexually arousing fantasies involving sexual activity with a prepubescent child or children (generally age 13 or younger). The person has acted on these urges, or is markedly distressed by them" (p 285).

Despite the continual changes in the conceptualization of paraphiliac disorder illustrated in these DSM revisions, the current DSM-III-R definitions and diagnostic criteria continue to generate discussion.[10] Clinicians attempting to diagnose paraphilia are likely to find particularly troubling the criterion of "recurrent intense sexual urges and sexually arousing fantasies," and the criterion that "the person has acted on these urges or is markedly distressed by them." Because persons having paraphiliac disorders, especially those sex offenders identified by the criminal justice system and seen for psychiatric evaluation, tend to deny or at least minimize the extent of their sexually perverse behavior, these criteria pose serious difficulties for the clinician. As Abel et al[11] have pointed out, denial is extremely common among sex offenders; it is, in fact, their "most commonly used defense: conscious or unconscious" (p 298). By obtaining a Certificate of Confidentiality for their outpatient sex offenders, Abel et al found that the extent of these patients' criminal sexual behaviors was considerably greater than they acknowledged before obtaining a guarantee of confidentiality. It should be noted, too, that these investigators also conceded that they were able to elicit these (probably more accurate) accounts from these sex offenders for two additional reasons: they spent up to five hours with each man to enhance rapport, and they asked them very specific questions about each paraphiliac behavior to obtain detailed answers. Among the principal conclusions of their study of 561 men seen in their clinic were that (1) the majority of paraphiliacs could have sex with adult partners without resorting to paraphiliac fantasies, (2) deviant and nondeviant sexual behavior occurred in most of these men, (3) most paraphiliacs engage in many different types of deviant sexual behavior, and (4) concomitantly, the paraphiliac with only one deviant sexual behavior is rare.

If accurate information about paraphiliac acts is difficult to ascertain, the criterion concerning deviant sexual fantasies is even more troublesome. As regards the significance of deviant sexual fantasies, Conte,[12] for example, not only raises questions about the actual prevalence of these fantasies among sex offenders, but he also questions whether such fantasies occur more commonly among sex offenders than among sexually nondeviant individuals. Clearly, much more research is needed here, as in the entire area of deviant sexuality. Our own experience evaluating sex offenders in a court clinic during the postconviction stage (when individuals would be expected to be less fearful of disclosure) indicates that sex offenders do experience recurrent deviant sexual fantasies and urges, but most will not reveal them until later on in the treatment phase.[10] Consequently, the DSM-III-R criteria for the diagnosis of paraphilia would most likely not be met on initial examination in many, if not in most, cases. It should be emphasized that even if the individual admits having engaged in deviant sexual behavior, this does not mean that he will reveal its true extent or compulsive nature, and he is even less likely to describe his recurrent fantasies and urges. The reason for this probably stems from the individual's capacity to cognitively distort or engage in faulty thinking about his paraphiliac behavior. He may be able, for example, to deceive himself to some degree by maintaining that he committed the unlawful sexual acts because he was under the influence of alcohol. However, when the individual admits to fantasies and urges, he is forced to confront the reality of his problem and to acknowledge some degree of responsibility for his behavior. In general, we have found that patients progress slowly from some acknowledgment of a paraphiliac problem (an acknowledgment that frequently occurs only after patients are confronted with the results of their erection measurement studies),[13] to an acknowledgment of the compulsive nature of the behavior, and, only if successfully engaged in treatment, to the patient's revelation of details about fantasies and urges.[10]

Other noteworthy changes in the DSM-III-R further highlights the role of contemporary perception in the diagnosis and classification of sexually deviant behaviors. Zoophilia is no longer included as a separate diagnostic category, because, the DSM-III-R announces, it is no longer considered to be a "clinically significant problem by itself" (p 425); instead, it is included in the category of "Paraphilia Not Otherwise Specified." Incest is introduced as a subtype of pedophilia, probably because of increasing reports that a small minority of incest offenders also victimize children outside of their families.[14] Moreover, in a comparative study of the erection measurements of incest offenders and heterosexual pedophiles, Abel et al[15] concluded that "the so-called cases of heterosexual incest are not different in their sexual preferences from heterosexual pedophiles since both groups are highly aroused by young children other than relatives" (p 136). Significantly, compulsive rape continues to be excluded as a paraphiliac disorder. Abel and Rouleau[16] attribute this to the fact that psychiatrists and psychologists have little contact with and therefore limited information about the more aggressive sex offenders; they point out that the more aggressive the sex crime is the more likely the offender is to be seen by society as in need of punishment rather than treatment, and add that the classification of rape as a paraphiliac disorder would constitute a setback to the women's movement. Other changes of particular interest in the DSM-III-R include the placement of "Gender Identity Disorders" in the childhood section because these disorders are now considered to arise in childhood. And although "Ego-dystonic Homosexuality" was eliminated as a distinct category, it could be included in the new category of "Sexual Disorder, Not Otherwise Specified" if it met the DSM-III criteria for "Ego-dystonic Homosexuality."

TYPOLOGICAL AND CLASSIFICATORY CONSIDERATIONS

Despite the general recognition that persons engaging in sexually perverse behaviors constitute a heterogeneous group, researchers are continually attempting to find common identifiable characteristics in these individuals.[10] Knight et al[17] assert that by choosing crucial, discriminating variables and discarding irrelevant ones, the usefulness of the typological scheme for sex offenders can be increased. The authors review the data, methods, and perspectives that provide the basis for the existing clinical typologies and examine the commonalities among these systems to determine whether they reveal any consistent types. Knight et al[17] describe how rapists and child molesters have been investigated from basically four major perspectives: sociological approaches that focused on the chain of events with a sociocultural context (such as the sequence of interaction between victims and offender in Amir's[18] study of rape in Philadelphia); legal and psychiatric approaches that use the individual's legal classification as the basis of placement in a subgroup of sex offenders and then use such established psychiatric systems as the DSM-I, II, or III to diagnose them; psychometric approaches that describe sex offenders through a multitude of self-report and projective techniques; and physiological/behavioral approaches that attempt to diagnose subgroups of sex offenders based upon their erection measurement studies. These authors conclude by outlining both the rational and the empirical strategies that could advance the field of typological classification.

Using these combined strategies in complementary ways, efforts have been undertaken to develop taxonomic systems for classifying sex offenders, especially rapists and child molesters. As Prentky et al[19] have stated, "the general purpose of this taxonomy is to reduce heterogeneity through the development of discrete, coherent subgroups" (p 43). Since most of this research is conducted at the Massachusetts Treatment Center for Sexually Dangerous Persons in Bridgewater, Massachusetts, the child molester and rapist typologies, each of which have gone through two revisions, are known as the Massachusetts Treatment Center: Child Molester Typology One, Two, and Three (MTC:CM1, MTC:CM2, and MTC:CM3); and the Massachusetts Treatment Center: Rapist Typology One, Two, and Three (MTC:R1, MTC:R2, and MTC:R3).[20] The taxonomic scheme for child molesters is derived from the model suggested by Cohen et al[21] of four types of child molesters—fixated, regressed, exploitative, and aggressive or sadistic.[22] This led to the eight-group typology of MTC:CM2. The second revision, MTC:CM3, consists of assessing the sex offender on two separate axes. Axis I involves decisions on two independent constructs: fixation and social competence. Axis II involves decisions about whether or not there is a high amount of contact with children, which subdivides into a decision of interpersonal or narcissistic meaning to the contact and a low amount of contact, leading to further decisions on low or high physical injury, this last again subdivided into sadistic or nonsadistic. By crossing the four types of Axis I with the six types of Axis II, a total of 24 combinations is possible. Knight and Prentky explain their judicious use of two axes as essential because of the uncertainty about the precise interrelationships among the Axis I and II variables. Similarly, the taxonomy for rapists stems from the original description by Cohen et al[23] of four types of rapists differentiated from one another by the relative motivations of sex and aggression. These four types are the displaced-aggression type, the compensatory type, the sex-aggression-diffusion type, and the impulse type. The revised MTC:R3 typology includes four categories at the top of the system which describe four primary motivations for rape: the opportunistic type, divided into either the high or low social competence group; the pervasively angry type; the sexual type, divided into a sadistic group further subdivided according to the presence or absence of sadistic fantasies, and a nonsadistic group, subdivided according to high or low social competence; and finally, the vindictive type, which is divided into low or moderate social competence. Knight and Prentky[20] believe that their taxonomic system for child molesters has demonstrated reasonable reliability and that "aspects of the model have important prognostic implications," although they caution that, "in contrast, our recently refined typological model for rapists remains untested" (p 48). These researchers underscore the need for further data to validate the taxonomic scheme for rapists, and they emphasize the importance of simultaneously employing both deductive-rational and inductive-empirical research strategies.

PERSONALITY FACTORS IN SEXUAL PERVERSIONS

Although the DSM-II-R diagnosis of paraphiliac disorder, as was pointed out above, is now made independently of personality considerations, the question of whether or not these individuals have common personality characteristics continues to generate discussion.[10] Earlier researchers had attempted to find identifiable, characterological traits within special groups of sexually deviant individuals such as pedophiles and exhibitionists. Frosch and Bromberg,[24] for example, described a variety of behavioral characteristics, including immaturity, emotional instability, and schizoid personality that are found among pedophiles. In his book, *The Sexual Offender and His Offenses*, published in 1954, Karpman[25] described some of the varying findings by researchers on the degree of psychopathology found among sex offenders grouped according to their sexual offenses. Summarizing the existing literature on exhibitionists, for example, Karpman wrote that "there is general agreement as to the lack of aggressiveness, inferiority, timidity, and heterosexual immaturity of the exhibitionist" (p 208). Among several writers that Karpman cited on this subject is Rickles,[26] who believed exhibitionists to be "compulsive neurotics, basing this diagnosis upon the finding that the exhibitionist is rigid, isolated, sheltered, orderly, and ... [displays] anal characteristics ... " (p 209). Significantly, Karpman believed that sexual perversions "are forms and expressions of neuroses," and that "paraphiliac neuroses differ from hysterical neuroses in that the paraphiliac is conscious of being different sexually, while in the hysterical neurotic the paraphilias remain repressed ... " (p 47).

Based upon their study of pedophiliac offenders seen at the New Jersey State Diagnostic Center for a psychiatric-psychological evaluation, Revitch and Weiss[27] concluded that "pedophilia is most likely to occur in certain types of personality organization" and is "more common in those individuals who are emotionally immature, physically underdeveloped, or have physical and mental defects" (p 75). In their book *Pedophilia and Exhibitionism*, published in 1964, Mohr et al[28] emphasize that existing research data indicate that, among pedophilic offenders, psychosis is rare, mental defectives are uncommon, and most of the psychiatric symptoms are related to such personality deficiencies as "immaturity, inadequacy, and schizoid withdrawal" (p 90). When these researchers gave additional diagnoses to the exhibitionists they examined in the Forensic Clinic of the Toronto Psychiatric Hospital, they found that "the categories simply underline the concept of the exhibitionist as a person suffering from feelings of inadequacy and showing signs of immaturity in social relations" (p 161). Based on the 1605 cases of sex offenders committed to the Wisconsin State Department of public welfare for psychiatric evaluation under the Wisconsin Sex Crimes Law from 1951 through 1960, Pacht et al[29] concluded that as a group these offenders had functioned as "inadequate individuals ... impulse-ridden" with "overwhelming passive needs" (p 804). Moreover, Pacht et al wrote that "many of these individuals would fall into the category of ambulatory schizophrenic or borderline states" (p 805).

In contrast, other writers have been increasingly commenting on the lack of specificity of characterological traits among sexually deviant individuals. As early as 1951, Bowman[30] pointed out that "sexual psychology is but one aspect of the whole personality and any type of treatment must take into account the total personality" (pp 255–256). Similarly, Cormier,[31] in 1972, wrote that "to understand the sex offense with all its implications, psychiatrists must see the offender as a total man ... " (p 48). In regard to the child molester, Quinsey[32] emphasized that "the selection of a child as a sexual object is [not] necessarily a reflection of some enduring character trait or disposition on the part of the offender" (p 205). Likewise, Conte[33] has asserted that "there is no currently verified profile of the typical adult who sexually abuses children" (p 345). In a study of cases of sexual deviation associated with personality disorder, Schmidt et al[34] concluded that "the degree of sexual deviance (frequency of acts, psychological investment) is not a function of the severity of the personality disorder, and the paraphilias are associated with various types of personality disorders" (p 286). Schmidt et al conclude that all the paraphiliac cases studied suggest that these individuals "have some degree of pathology, most usually in the area of their capacity for intimate mutual relationships," but quickly go on to note that "the degree of character pathology varies considerably from patient to patient" (p 294). In fact, as Gabbard[35] asserts, "A wide range of psychiatric diagnoses and levels of personality organization may be present in someone with a paraphilia" (p 231).

CONCLUSION

This discussion on the diagnosis and classification of sexual perversions highlights and is representative of a basic conceptual question about behavioral disorders in general: is the paraphilia merely an aberrant behavior in an otherwise normal individual, or is the sexual perversion a symptomatic expression of profound characterological pathology? Behaviorally oriented and psychodynamically oriented therapists are concerned with this question because it bears directly on their treatment approaches to removing what is conceptualized as either a troubling behavior or a symptom. Complicating the entire matter is the fact that sexually perverse behavior has been shown to cut across different personality types and diagnostic entities. Furthermore, most researchers attribute complex, multiple factors, including biological, learning-behavioral, psychodynamic, and sociocultural factors as etiologic of paraphilia. The same factors may contribute in uncertain ways to the development of underlying character structure. Consequently, clinicians must evaluate the uniqueness of each paraphiliac patient in order to understand and to be able to more effectively treat the patient.

REFERENCES

1. Travin S, Bluestone H, Coleman K, Melella J. Pedophilia: an update on theory and practice. *Psychiatr Q.* 1985;57:80–103.
2. Spitzer RL, Williams JBW. Classification of mental disorders. In: Kaplan HI, Sadock BJ eds. *Comprehensive Textbook of Psychiatry, 1.* 4th ed. Baltimore, Md: Williams & Wilkins; 1985.
3. American Psychiatric Association. *Diagnostic and Statistical Manual of Mental Disorders (DSM-I).* Washington, DC: American Psychiatric Association; 1968.
4. American Psychiatric Association. *Diagnostic and Statistical Manual of Mental Disorders (DSM-II).* 2nd ed. Washington, DC: American Psychiatric Association; 1968.
5. Klerman GL. Classification and DSM-III-R. In: Nicholai Jr AM, ed. *The New Harvard Guide to Psychiatry.* Cambridge, Mass: The Belknap Press of Harvard University Press; 1988.
6. American Psychiatric Association. *Diagnostic and Statistical Manual of Mental Disorders (DSM-III).* 3rd ed. Washington, DC: American Psychiatric Association; 1980.
7. Quinesy VL. The assessment and treatment of child molesters. *Canad Psych Rev.* 1977, 18:204–220.
8. Meyer JK. Paraphilias. In: Kaplan HI, Sadock BJ, eds. *Comprehensive Textbook of Psychiatry, I.* 4th ed. Baltimore, Md: Williams & Wilkins; 1985.
9. American Psychiatric Association. *Diagnostic and Statistical Manual of Mental Disorders—Revised (DSM-III-R).* 3rd ed, revised. Washington, DC: American Psychiatric Association; 1987.
10. Travin S. The use of psychiatric expertise in sex offender cases. In: Rosner R, Weinstock R, eds. *Ethical Practice in Psychiatry and the Law.* New York, NY: Plenum Press; 1990; 262–292.
11. Abel GG, Becker, JV, Cunningham-Rathner J, Mittelman M, Rouleau JL. Multiple paraphilic diagnoses among sex offenders. *Bull Am Acad Psychiatry Law.* 1988;16:153–168.
12. Conte JR. Clinical dimensions of adult sexual abuse of children. *Behav Sci Law.* 1985;3:341–354.
13. Travin S, Cullen K, Melella JT. The use and abuse of erection measurements: a forensic perspective. *Bull Am Acad Psychiatry Law.* 1988;16:235–250.
14. Langevin R, Day D, Handy L, Russon AE. Are incestuous fathers pedophilic, aggressive, and alcoholic? In: Langevin R, ed. *Erotic Preference, Gender Identity, and Aggression in Men: New Research Studies.* Hillside, NJ: Lawrence Erlbaum Associates Publishers; 1985.
15. Abel GG, Becker JV, Murphy WD, Flanagan, B. Identifying dangerous child molesters. In: Stuart R, ed. *Violent Behavior: Social Learning Approaches to Prediction, Management and Treatment.* New York, NY: Brunner/Mazel; 1981.
16. Abel GG, Rouleau JL. The nature and extent of sexual assault. In: Marshall WL, Laws DR, Barbaree HE, eds. *Handbook of Sexual Assault: Issues, Theories, and Treatment of the Offender.* New York, NY: Plenum Press; 1990.
17. Knight RA, Rosenberg R, Schneider BA. Classification of sexual offenders: perspectives, methods, and validation. In: Burgess AW, ed. *Rape and Sexual Assault: A Research Handbook.* New York, NY: Garland Publishing Inc, 1985.
18. Amir M. *Pattern in Forcible Rape.* Chicago, Ill: University of Chicago Press; 1971.

19. Prentky R, Cohen M, Seghorn T. Development of a rational taxonomy for the classification of rapists: the massachusetts treatment center. *Bull Am Acad Psychiatry Law.* 1985;1339-70.
20. Knight RA, Prentky R. Classifying sexual offenders: the development and corroboration of taxonomic models. In: Marshal WL, Laws DR, Barbaree HE, eds. *Handbook of Sexual Assault: Issues, Theories and Treatment of the Offender.* New York, NY: Plenum Press; 1990.
21. Cohen M, Boucher RJ, Seghorn TK, Mehegan J. *The Sexual Offender Against Children.* Presented at a meeting of the Association for Professional Treatment of Offenders. Boston, Mass: 1979.
22. Knight RA. A taxonomic analysis of child molesters. In: Prentky RA, Quinsey VL, eds. *Human Sexual Aggression: Current Perspectives. Annals of the New York Academy of Sciences.* Vol 528. New York, NY: The New York Academy of Science; 1998.
23. Cohen M, Seghorn T, Calmas W. Sociometric study of the sex offender. *J Abnorm Psych.* 1969;74:249-255.
24. Frosch J, Bromberg W. The sex offender: a psychiatric study. *Am J Orthopsychiatry.* 1939;9:761-776.
25. Karpman B. *The Sexual Offender and his Offenses: Etiology, Pathology, Psychodynamics and Treatment.* New York, NY: The Julian Press Inc, 1954.
26. Rickles NK. *Exhibitionism.* Philadelphia, PA. JB Lippincott Co; 1950.
27. Revitch E, Weiss RG. The pedophiliac offender. *Dis Nerv Syst.* 1962;23:73-78.
28. Mohr JW, Turner RE, Jerry MB. *Pedophilia and Exhibitionism.* Toronto, Canada: University of Toronto Press; 1964.
29. Pacht AR, Halleck SL, Ehrmann JC. Diagnosis and treatment of the sexual offender: a nine-year study. *Am J Psychiatry.* 1962;March;802-808.
30. Bowman KM. The problem of the sex offender. *Am Jour Psychiatry.* 1951;108:250-257.
31. Cormier BM. The dilemma of psychiatric diagnosis. In: Resnik HLP, Wolfgang ME, eds. *Sexual Behaviors: Social, Clinical, and Legal Aspects.* Boston, Mass: Little Brown & Co; 1972.
32. Quinsey VL. The assessment and treatment of child molesters, *Canad Psych Rev.* 1977;18:204-220.
33. Conte JR. Clinical dimensions of adult sexual abuse of children. *Behav Sci Law.* 1985;3:341-354.
34. Schmidt, CW, Meyer JK, Lucas J. Paraphilias and personality disorders. In: Lion JR, ed. *Personality Disorders: Diagnosis and Management.* (Revised for DSM-III.) 2nd ed. Baltimore, Md: Williams & Wilkins; 1981.
35. Gabbard GO. *Psychodynamic Psychiatry in Clinical Practice.* Washington, DC: American Psychiatric Press Inc; 1990.

4

Biological Perspectives on Sexual Perversion

The increasing concern about biological factors relevant to sexual perversions mirrors the growing recognition of the importance of biological factors to psychiatric disorders. Freud himself always maintained that biological factors would eventually be discovered that would contribute immensely to our understanding of psychological processes, including some physical and endocrinological factors; certainly, a number of biological factors have a bearing on sexual expression; nevertheless, we must always be mindful that, in as complex an organism as the human, sexual expression is influenced by many factors.[1] The need for consequent restraint in drawing conclusions based upon any one set of factors has particular relevance in the area of sexual perversion, because of its inherent vulnerability to misconceptions.

BIOLOGICAL FACTORS IN GENDER DEVELOPMENT

Because most individuals suffering from paraphiliac disorders are male, an increasing number of authors[2-4] have been considering a possible connection between male gender development gone awry and the susceptibility to form an aberrant sexual behavioral pattern. Gadpaille[2] has written that "the greater complexity of differentiation of the male fetus and fetal hypothalamus, including perhaps the delaying influence of the Y chromosome, helps to explain the higher incidence of paraphilias in males..." (p 11). In a similar vein, although focusing on a later stage of development, Stoller[3] has argued that a "buried unsureness of gender identity" lies at the roots of "the perversions" (p 18). In his recent *Gender Disorders and the Paraphilias*, Arndt[4] expresses surprise that so few books have been written on the subject, as he sees a commonality between the two: "not only gender disorders, but also the paraphilias, involve distortions in conception of masculinity and femininity..." (p X).

Contemporary discussions of biological factors in sexual perversions employ several key terms that we need to discuss before proceeding further, terms such as core gender identity, gender identity, and gender role. Despite considerable nosological confusion in this area, Money[5] has provided a brief historical account of the origins of these terms. While writing his dissertation on the psychology of hermaphroditism (inspired partly by Freud's mention of bisexuality in *Three Contributions to the Theory of Sex*), Money[6] used the term "gender role" as an all-inclusive term to refer to nonerotic and nongenital sex roles in order to distinguish the term from the mere sex of the genitalia and their functions. In a 1955 coauthored paper on hermaphroditism, Money et al[7] defined gender role as "all those things that a person says or does to disclose himself or herself as having the status of boy or man, girl or woman, respectively," and added that "it includes, but is not restricted to sexuality in the sense of eroticism" (p 302). Later, in his 1967 *Sex Research: New Developments*, Money[8] defined "gender identity" as "the sameness, unity, and persistence of one's individuality as male or female (or ambivalent)" and distinguished "gender identity" from "gender role": "Gender identity is the private experience of gender role, and gender role is the public expression of gender identity" (glossary). Stoller,[9] an eminent psychoanalyst with a profound interest in gender disorders, originated the term "core gender identity" defining it as "an unalterable sense of gender identity—a core gender identity ('I am male, I am female')," which is developed "by the time of the phallic stage" (p 223). Stoller believes that this core of gender awareness (ie, of being either a male or a female) starts very early in life and is produced by three basic elements: (1) "anatomy of the external genitalia," (2) "infant–parent relationships," and (3) a postulated "biological force" (p 223). According to Stoller,[3] core gender identity "is the first step in the progress towards one's ultimate gender identity and the nexus around which masculinity and femininity gradually accrete" (p 11). Similarly, Money and Ehrhardt[10] describe the entire process of gender identity differentiation as a process that involves complex and inseparable combinations of prenatal and even larger postnatal factors, each comprised of biological and psychological components and subject to innate and acquired influences.

Prenatal factors of sexual differentiation consist of the proper and sequential functioning of sex chromosomes and hormones. Because many of the studies on sex differences have been performed on lower animals, caution is clearly necessary in extrapolating from these findings to humans. "Sexual dimorphism" is the term usually used to refer to the manifest differences between males and females at either the morphological or the molecular level.[11] It is the male Y chromosome that determines testicular differentiation, or its absence that allows ovaries to develop. The different gonadal secretions account for the development of sexual dimorphism. Formerly, the number of chromosomes in the human cell was believed to be 48, but in 1956, after careful observation, Tjio and Levan[12] concluded that the actual number was 22 paired autosomes and additional X and Y sex chromosomes for a total of 46. In 1949, Barr and Bertram[13] discovered an extra piece of heterochromatin adjacent to the nuclear membrane in the neurons of female cats. Berlin[14] pointed out that this heterochromatin material could be part of the inactivated second X chromosome of females.[15] It is now called a Barr body, and can be tested for by buccal smears or skin biopsies. Berlin[14] cites another laboratory test that can be used to identify biological gender; it involves searching for a drumstick-like appendage in the neutrophil white blood cells of females.[16]

Throughout the first six weeks of fetal life there is no differentiation of the primitive gonads in both sexes. Then, during the seventh week, the putative testicular determining factors (TDF) cause testicular differentiation to occur.[17] Significantly, if the testicular determining factors are absent, the primitive gonads will proceed spontaneously to develop into ovaries. Bancroft[18] notes that, formerly, the "male determining factor was believed to be related to an antigen on the chromosome called the [histocompatibility] HY antigen . . . " But Bancroft goes on to say that "this now seems unlikely, although it is possible that different mechanisms are involved in the differentiation of somatic and germ cells" (pp 153–154). In the female, the primordial muellerian duct will give rise to the female genital structures. In the male, the primordial Wolffian duct will be stimulated by the testosterone secreted by the Leydig cells in the testes to develop into male internal genital structures. The differentiation of the male external genitalia and prostate gland requires that testosterone be converted by the enzyme 5 reductase into dihydrotestosterone. In 5 reductase deficiency, the individual will have normal Wolffian duct differentiation, but will fail to develop external male genitalia and the prostate gland. Male sexual development also fails in case of androgen receptor defects.[17]

The effects that the gonadal steroids have on the developing central nervous system are not fully known. What seems to be true is that there is a "critical period" in each species during which time the central nervous system is especially sensitive for sexual differentiation.[19] In his review of sex differences in the brain, McEwen[20] describes this critical period when testosterone secretion masculinizes and defeminizes structures throughout the brain and the reproductive organ, and concludes that "male and female brains begin postnatal life with subtle and functional differences that bias the input and output of information and modify experiences" (p 40).

Bancroft[18] delineates three main types of biological abnormalities in sexual development. The first type consists of sex chromosome abnormalities, including XO—gonadal dysgenesis or Turner's syndrome; XXX, or triple-X anomaly; XXY, or Klinefelter's syndrome; and XYY. The second category comprises inborn errors of metabolism, including androgen insensitivity syndrome (or testicular feminization syndrome); andrenogenital syndrome (congenital adrenal hyperplasia); and 5 reductase deficiency. The third type of abnormalities in sexual development are those caused by exposure to exogenous steroids during fetal development, including the effects of synthetic steroids administered to prevent spontaneous abortion, and the effects of giving estrogens or estrogen/progestogen combinations to diabetic women during pregnancy. Bancroft concludes that, though learning probably plays the major role in sexual preference, "underlying this learning we must nevertheless allow for some biologically determined predisposition, particularly in relation to our preference for male or female partners" (p 196). Arndt[4] too notes that biological forces are not by themselves decisive in influencing sexuality, but believes that "the most probable biological influence on sexuality is the effect of prenatal hormones that tend to demasculinize the baby boy both in body conformation and in the hypothalamic-pituitary-neuroendocrine function and hemispheric lateralization" (p 398).

Although Berlin[14] cautions us about reaching conclusions regarding a relationship between Klinefelter's syndrome and sexual deviation, he nevertheless believes that a review of the literature suggests that the "prevalence of sexual deviation syndromes in Klinefelter's patients may indeed be higher than it is amongst non-Klinefelter's men" (p 96). About 1 in 700 males are born with the characteristic extra X chromosome and a 47,XXY karyotype.[18] Nielsen[21] surveyed 48 studies of groups of males with Klinefelter's syndrome and found that out of 411 males in these studies, 15 (3.6%) were homosexuals, 10 (2.4%) transvestites, 8 (1.9%) pedophiles, and 2 (0.5%) had other sexual perversions. Nielsen[22] believed that the 47,XXY chromosome configuration in Klinefelter's syndrome may be one of the etiological factors in the development of gender role and gender identity problems in these males. But the primary etiology, he concluded, is probably a defect occurring in the early years of gender role and identity development that contributes to the parents' attitude toward their sons. Berlin,[14] on the other hand, points out that "since most Klinefelter's patients appear to be essentially normal boys until puberty, it is difficult to account for this apparently high prevalence of sexual deviation on the basis of child rearing practices or other types of early life experiences" (p 96). Because Klinefelter's patients at birth appear to be males, their parents routinely assign and rear them as boys. Significantly, some of these boys, even at an early age, may begin to have gender feelings of being female. In adolescence, the typical gynecomastia and specific type of hypogonadism with spermatogenesis, increased excretion of follicle-stimulating hormone and reduced excretion of 17-ketosteroids,[23] as well as other physical and laboratory findings confirm the diagnosis of Klinefelter's.[14]

PLASMA TESTOSTERONE LEVELS AND SEXUAL AGGRESSION

The relationship between plasma testosterone levels and sexual aggression has been the subject of considerable research. The finding of correlations between the two would have important implications for treatment. However, despite intensive efforts, researchers have not been able to show consistent correlations.

Basic physiologic data specify that testosterone is mainly secreted by the interstitial (Leydig cells) of the testes, and is the principal androgenic steroid in the plasma of males. Before pubescence, plasma testosterone concentration is less than 20 ng/dl; in the adult male it is 300–1000 ng/dl. About 98% of testosterone is bound to several different proteins in the plasma, and the remaining 2%, which is free, accounts for the principal androgenic effects.[24]

The anterior pituitary gland secretes two gonadotropins—the luteinizing hormone (LH), also named interstitial cell-stimulating hormone, and the follicle-stimulating hormone (FSH).[17] This secretion is under the control of the gonadotropin-releasing hormone (GnRH), which is produced in the hypothalamus and transported through a special portal circulation. Additional regulation of this pituitary gonadotropin secretion is performed by such testis substances as inhibin and gonadal steroids. The LH pituitary gonadotropin is released into the bloodstream and binds onto specific membrane receptors of the Leydig cells in the testis leading to the biosynthesis of testosterone. Further LH gonadotropin production is inhibited by the action of testicular androgens in the central nervous system and the pituitary. West[17] commented that "LH-producing pituitary cells and androgen-producing Leydig cells form a closed-loop axis" (p 855). The FSH pituitary gonadotropin that is released binds onto specific membrane receptors of Sertoli cells situated inside the seminiferous tubules of the testis. Sertoli cells are the chief regulators of spermatogenesis. Inhibin, a protein produced by the Sertoli cells, contributes another closed-loop feedback system with the pituitary FSH-producing cells. Thus, there are dynamic, closed-feedback mechanisms on the hypothalamic pituitary-testis axis that regulate serum levels of testicular hormones and reproductive functions.[17]

In a study of a possible hypothalamic-pituitary-gonadal axis dysfunction in pedophiles, Gaffney and Berlin[25] compared the effects of an infusion of 100 mcg of synthetic luteinizing hormone-releasing hormone (LHRH) into 7 pedophilic men, 5 other-type paraphiliac men, and 5 controls. The findings showed a marked elevation of luteinizing hormone (LH) in the pedophilic men compared with the other paraphiliacs and controls. The results in the pedophiles were comparable to the responses in some patients with Klinefelter's syndrome, suggesting some kind of pathophysiological significance. Although this was only a preliminary study, Gaffney and Berlin believe their findings indicate hypothalamic-pituitary-gonadal dysfunction in this group of pedophilic men. However, these authors also acknowledge that an earlier study by Buhrich et al[26] did not find any abnormal LH or FSH hormonal levels in transvestite men.

Plasma testosterone levels and their relationship to sexual stimulation have been studied in normal men. In a study of a normal male subjects' testosterone levels during and immediately after sexual intercourse, Fox et al[27] found significantly increased levels. There were no such increased testosterone levels among seven subjects during masturbation. Rubin et al[28] measured the penile erectile responses to erotic films of six sexually nondeviant men and found that their "sexual arousal and sexual arousability" (p 310) were significantly correlated with fluctuations in their endogenous plasma testosterone concentrations. They also found a significant inverse relationship between testosterone levels and frequency of reported orgasms in these men preceding the experimental sessions. Bancroft[18] cites other conflicting findings including the finding by Purvis et al[29] of a rise in testosterone levels following masturbation, and failure by Stearn et al[30] to find significant hormonal changes following coitus and masturbation. Bancroft concludes that "there are clearly no simple predictable effects of sexual activity on hormonal levels in men" (p 100).

Plasma testosterone levels among sex offenders have shown equally conflicting findings. Rada[31] investigated the plasma testosterone levels of 52 rapists and 12 child molesters and found them to be within normal ranges. Higher mean testosterone levels were found among the violent rapists, and the highest testosterone level (1236 ng/100 ml) occurred in the one rapist who had killed his victim. However, in another study, Rada[32] found that rapists' levels of testosterone were higher than those of child molesters and controls, that violent and nonviolent rapists' levels were comparable, and that the highest levels occurred among violent child molesters. Rada[33] has concluded that "our knowledge of the effects of androgen hormone on the forms of sexual expression and on the commission of aggressive acts remains rudimentary" (p 463). On his use of medication to treat deviant sexual disorders, Berlin[14] comments that "the use of biological methods to successfully treat a condition does not prove that the condition and the treatment are directly and simply related" (p 103).

Medroxyprogesterone acetate (MPA, or Depo-Provera), a synthetic progesterone manufactured by the Upjohn Pharmaceutical Company, is the drug most frequently used in the experimental treatment of paraphiliac disorders in this country.[34] MPA decreases plasma testosterone level, mostly by the induction of testosterone-A-reductase in the liver, but also by affecting its production rate and increasing its clearance rate. The drug also has antigonadotropic effects, and competes with androgens at their receptors.[35] Cooper[36] points out that most investigators who used the drug observed significant decreases in sexual tension, fantasies, and preoccupation in their paraphiliac patients.

BRAIN DAMAGE, DYSFUNCTION, AND TEMPORAL LOBE DISORDERS

An apparent association between brain damage or abnormalities in brain functioning and aberrant sexual behavior has been the subject of a number of reports in the literature. Regenstein and Reich[37] have reported the cases of four married men, ranging in age from 31 to 56, who first manifested pedophilic behavior after suffering illnesses that resulted in cognitive impairments. The first man had a meningioma removed by right frontal craniotomy; the second suffered a severe myocardial infarction with ventricular fibrillation requiring cardioversion and later cardiac surgery; the third also suffered an acute myocardial infarction necessitating resuscitation and subsequent cardiac surgery; and the fourth had progressive neurological impairments with a possible diagnosis of vestibular neuronitis. These authors conclude that "when pedophilia arises in patients without evidence of previous sexual perversion, a careful investigation of nervous system functioning seems warranted" (p 798). Cooper[38] reports on four cases of institutionalized male patients who had varying degrees of dementia and were engaging in genital exposure, compulsive masturbation, and other disruptive sexual behavior. These patients could not be managed by other means, but responded to medroxyprogesterone acetate (MPA) treatment within two weeks of administration. Hucker and Ben-Aron[39] believe that sex offenses, and especially pedophilic acts, committed for the first time by men over 60 years of age, who have no prior history of sexual perversion, may be explained also in psychosocial terms. Although theorists have usually attributed sex offenses committed by older men to senile dementia, a contributory psychosocial factor may exist in such cases: "loneliness and isolation might affect the judgment of these men so that they act upon deviant impulses that they normally kept under better control" (p 221).

In a pilot study to investigate possible brain damage among six cases of men designated as mentally disordered sex offenders under the Nebraska Penal Code, Graber et al[40] utilized the Luria-Nebraska Neuropsychological Battery, computed tomography scan measure, and regional cerebral blood flow analysis. Their preliminary findings were that 50% of these offenders "showed brain dysfunction as demonstrated by decreased density measure, decreased blood flow and performance deficits on the Luria Battery" (p 125). Scott et al[41] also administered the Luria-Nebraska Neuropsychological Battery to 36 male patients who were arrested for sexual assault in Nebraska and required to undergo evaluation as possible "mentally disordered sex offenders." According to the investigators, the results indicated that many of these men suffered from cerebral dysfunction. In a study of 16 incarcerated male pedophiles, Hendricks et al[42] essentially replicated the earlier studies and found that "compared with controls, child molesters... have thinner and less dense skulls and lower rcBF [regional cerebral blood flow] values" (p 108).

Temporal lobe disorders have been observed to be related to changes in sexual behavior.[43] Blumer[43] has cited Kluver and Bucy's[44] research on the removal of the temporal lobes in rhesus monkeys that resulted in drastic changes in their sexual behavior. The monkeys became markedly hypersexual, with an accompanying decrease in anger and fear. The limbic region in the medial temporal portion was believed to be responsible for these behavioral changes. The Kluver-Bucy, or temporal lobe syndrome, may be observed in humans following removal of both anterior temporal lobes.[45]

In a comprehensive survey of the literature, Langevin[46] has concluded "that there are suggestions that the temporal lobes of the brain are most often linked with sexual behavior" (p 103), and added that "there is some suggestion that sadists and pedophiles show differential brain pathology in the temporal lobes, with the former showing structural anomalies to the right lobe, while the pedophiles appear to have anomalies in the left lobe" (p 112).

In regard to temporal lobe (psychomotor) epilepsy, Blumer[47] cites Gastaut and Collomb's[48] observation that this disorder is marked by global hyposexuality, with reduction in both libidinal and genital functioning in more than half of the patients studied. In a series of 50 patients of both sexes having temporal lobe epilepsy, of whom 42 had unilateral temporal lobectomies, Blumer[47] described 29 (58%) of them as showing global hyposexuality and 7 (14%) as having distinct episodes of hypersexuality. In six of these patients, the hypersexual episodes had occurred after the abrupt termination of the temporal lobe seizure activity. Blumer believes that these findings demonstrate "the role of the temporal limbic structures in the regulation of sexual arousal" (p 1105).

Additionally, Blumer[43] cites a number of studies that have pointed out an occasional connection between temporal lobe epilepsy or abnormalities and deviant sexual behavior, particularly transvestism and fetishism. Among these studies is that of Davies and Morgenstern[49] who described a case of transvestism, which began in middle life following the onset of both grand mal and temporal lobe seizures. In 1961, Epstein[50] described five cases of either fetishism or transvestism, or both. Three of these cases manifested electroencephalographic abnormalities, one a suggestion of temporal abnormality, and the fifth one a generalized brain dysfunction. In 1967, Kolarsky et al[51] studied a group of 86 male patients, and concluded that temporal lobe damage had to be present since early childhood in order to be causally related to the development of a sexual deviation. Bancroft[18] writes that the "connections between epilepsy and sexual disturbances are likely to be complex" (p 572) for a variety of reasons, including social stigma, lack of self-confidence, and fear of failure—conditions more likely to affect the vulnerable child before sexual maturity has been attained.[52]

ALCOHOL AND SEXUAL ASSAULT

Because sex offenders frequently report drinking at the time of the commission of the offense, a connection between alcohol and sexual aggression has been considered. Among 77 rapists committed to Atascadero State Hospital in California, Rada[53] found that 50% of them were drinking at the time of the crime and that 35% could be diagnosed as alcoholics. Rada suggested two basic theories to explain the relationship between alcohol and sexual assault: the disinhibition theory and the theory that alcohol directly affects the brain centers for sexual and aggressive behavior. In another paper on alcohol and rape, Rada[54] speculated for heuristic reasons that for a small number of men alcohol may stimulate a different set of sexual fantasies and sensations, hence a special category of "alcohol-triggered rape" (p 58). In a study published in 1978, Rada et al[55] presented additional data on the drinking patterns of 382 sex offenders sent to Atascadero State

Hospital. The researchers found that 53% of the sex offenders reported drinking during the commission of the offense, most of them to a heavy or moderate degree. Although Rada et al[55] emphasize that the data do not prove a causal relationship, nevertheless, they note that "a number of factors suggest that alcohol may be more directly causal in child molestation than in rape" (p 299).

In order to determine the role of alcohol in facilitating sexual arousal, a number of studies have been conducted that essentially compare the penile erectile responses of subjects who were given alcohol to control subjects who were not given alcohol. Briddel et al[56] found that it was not the alcohol that produced the erectile response to rape cues in subjects, but rather the thought that they had drunk alcohol that accounted for greater sexual arousal. On the other hand, Barbaree et al,[57] utilizing a similar balanced-placebo design in their study, found that subjects who were intoxicated had difficulty in discriminating between nonconsenting and consenting cues, in contrast to subjects who had not ingested alcohol. Barbaree[58] believes that "alcohol intoxication might facilitate sexual assault by reducing men's sensitivity to societal demands for appropriate behavior" (p 131). In a study of the effects of alcohol on penile tumescense in 48 paid volunteers, Langevin et al[59] found "more or less indiscriminate reactions to erotica by drinking subjects," which led them to believe that "alcohol in general may serve a disinhibiting facilitative role in sexual arousal" (p 109). Langevin et al conclude that their findings suggest that sex offenders who blame their behavior on drinking cannot be routinely dismissed as lying.

DEPRESSION, OBSESSIVE-COMPULSIVE DISORDER, PARAPHILIA, AND NONPARAPHILIAC SEXUAL ADDICTION

Some recently published articles have suggested possible relationships between depression and paraphiliac disorder[60-61] or nonparaphiliac sexual addiction,[62] and between obsessive-compulsive disorder (OCD) and paraphiliac disorder.[63] In 1975, Ward[60] described a case of a 24-year-old man with a four and a half-year history of manic depression and a two-year history of tranvestism, which disappeared after lithium treatment. Ward explained that dynamically the tranvestism had been maintained by mood-dependent motives that were eliminated with the medication. By treating the identified underlying manic depression, the overt psychopathological syndrome (transvestism) could be alleviated. More recently, Kafka[61] has pointed out that there is a high incidence of major affective disorder in males with paraphiliac disorder. Kafka[62] has also underscored that some paraphiliac disorders and nonparaphiliac sexual addictions associated with depressive symptomatology can be successfully treated with antidepressant medications. Nonparaphiliac sexual addictions, which may be categorized according to the DSM-III-R as "Sexual Disorders Not Otherwise Specified," have generated some debate as to "whether the form of these behaviors constitutes an addiction, a compulsion, forms of hypersexuality, or a disorder of impulse control" (p 60). Kafka[62] suggests that in some cases of paraphilia or nonparaphiliac addictions, "the behavior can be conceptualized as a sexual dysregulation disorder in comorbid association with a mood disorder" (p 63). This relationship of sexual disorders to depression would be analogous to the relationship that bulimia nervosa, an eating dysregulation disorder, has to mood disorders.

Carnes,[64] who has popularized a treatment program for sexual addiction based on the Twelve Steps of Alcoholics Anonymous, views the sexual addict as operating at one or more of three levels of behaviors. Level 1 contains relatively acceptable compulsive sexual behaviors such as excessive masturbation and pornography usage, Level 2 has clear victimizing behaviors such as exhibitionism and voyeurism, and Level 3 has severe victimizing behaviors such as child molestation and rape.

Perilstein et al[63] have described three cases of paraphilias that were treated successfully with fluoxetine (Prozac), one of a pedophilia, the second of exhibitionism, and the third of voyeurism/frotteurism. Significantly, although all three patients acknowledged feelings of irritability, two of them denied being depressed or having vegetative symptoms, and could not be diagnosed as having a mood disorder. Perilstein et al[63] believe that "there may be more commonality among the paraphilias and obsessive compulsive disorders than has recently been acknowledged" (p 170). Fluoxatine, clomipramine, and fluvoxamine are all antidepressant drugs that have been shown to reduce the intensity of obsessive compulsive symptoms in patients who are not depressed.[65] The drugs seem to work in part by inhibiting the uptake of serotonin (5 hydroxytryptamine, 5-HT) from the synaptic space, and thus allowing more serotonin to be available in the postsynaptic receptors. It should be pointed out that, although serotonin appears to be involved in the mechanism of antiobsessional drug action, there is no clear evidence linking serotonin etiologically to the pathophysiology of obsessive-compulsive disorder.[65]

CONCLUSION

This chapter has basically reviewed some of the key biological factors believed to be relevant to sexual perversion. As in so many other areas of biopsychiatric research, the accumulated data on deviant sexuality may suggest possibilities, and even probabilities, but does not permit definite conclusions. This is partly because much of the brain research relating to sexuality is carried out on animals, and the data is often extrapolated to humans. Moreover, as is apparent in the discussion above, myriad difficulties surround attempts to estimate the percentage of biological factors contributing to the manifest behavior in comparison to the psychological and sociological factors influencing the sexual disorder. Furthermore, treatment responses to such drugs as androgen-depleting agents and antidepressants do not confirm the biophysiologic basis of paraphiliac disorders. Further research to clarify the contribution that biological factors make in the etiology, development, and manifestation of deviant sexuality is certainly warranted.

REFERENCES

1. Michael RP, Zumpe D. Biological factors in the organization and expression of sexual behavior. In: Rosen I, ed. *Sexual Deviation*. New York, NY: Oxford University Press; 1979.
2. Gadpaille WJ. Biological factors in the development of human sexual identity. In:

Meyer JK, ed. *Symposium on Sexuality. The Psychiatric Clinic of North America.* Vol 3. No. 1. Philadelphia, Pa: WB Saunders Co; April 1980.
3. Stoller RJ. *Presentations of Gender.* New Haven, Conn: Yale University Press; 1985.
4. Arndt WB. *Gender Disorder and the Paraphilias.* Madison, Conn: International Universities Press Inc; 1991.
5. Money J. Gender roles, gender identity, core gender identity: usage and definition of terms. *J Am Acad Psychoanal.* 1973;1:397–402.
6. Money J. *Hermaphroditism: An Inquiry into the Nature of a Human Paradox.* Ann Arbor, Mich: Harvard University Library; University Microfilms Library Services, Xerox Corporation; 1967. Doctoral dissertation.
7. Money J, Hampson JG, Hampson JL. An examination of some basic sexual concepts: the evidence of human hermaphroditism. *Bull Johns Hopkins Hospital.* 1955;97:301–319.
8. Money J, ed. *Sex Research: New Developments.* New York, NY: Holt, Rinehart & Winston; 1967.
9. Stoller R. A contribution to the study of gender identity. *Int J Psychoanal.* 1964;45:220–226.
10. Money J, Ehrhardt A. *Man and Woman, Boy and Girl: Differentiation and Dimorphism of Gender Identity from Conception to Maturity.* Baltimore, Md: The Johns Hopkins University Press; 1972.
11. Bardin CW, Catterall JF. Testosterone: a major determinant of extragenital sexual dimorphism. *Science.* 1981;211:1285–1294.
12. Tjio JH, Levan A. The chromosome number of man. *Hereditas.* 1956;42:1–6.
13. Barr MI, Bertram EG. A morphological distinction between neurones of the male and female and the behavior of the nucleolar satellite during accelerated nucleoprotein synthesis. *Nature.* 1949;163:676–677.
14. Berlin FS. Sex offenders: a biomedical perspective and a status report on biomedical treatment. In: Greer JG, Stuart IR, eds. *The Sexual Aggressor: Current Perspectives on Treatment.* New York, NY: Van Nostrand; 1983.
15. Lyon MF. X-Chromosome inactivation and development patterns in mammals. *Biological Review. Cambridge Philosophical Society,* Cambridge, Mass: 1972;47:1–35.
16. Kosek, MS. Medical genetics. In: Krupp MA, Chattum M, eds. *Current Diagnosis and Treatment.* Los Altos, Calif: Lange Medical Publications; 1972:883–884.
17. West JB, ed. *Best and Taylor's Physiological Basis of Medical Practice.* 12th ed. Baltimore, Md: Williams & Wilkins; 1991.
18. Bancroft J. *Human Sexuality and its Problems.* 22nd ed. Edinburgh, England: Churchill Livingstone; 1989.
19. MacLusky NJ, Naftolin F. Sexual differentiation of the central nervous system. *Science.* 1981;211:1294–1303.
20. McEwen BS. Sex differences in the brain: what they are and how they arise. In: Notman NIT, Nadelson CC, eds. *Women and Men: New Perspectives on Gender Differences.* Washington, DC: American Psychiatric Press Inc; 1991.
21. Nielsen J. Klinefelter's syndrome and the XYY syndrome. *Acta Psychiatric Scand.* 1969; (suppl 209) 13–353.
22. Nielsen J: Gender role-identity and sexual behavior in persons with sex chromosome aberrations. *Dan Med Bull* 1972;19:269–275.
23. Klinefelter HF, Reifenstein EC, Albright F. Syndrome characterized by gynecomastia, aspermatogenesis without A-leydigism and increased excretion of follicle stimulating hormone. *J Clin Endocrinol.* 1942;2:615–627.

24. Murand F, Haynes RC. Androgens. In: Gilman AG, Goodman LS, Rall TW, Murad F, eds. *Goodman and Gilman's the Pharmacological Basis of Therapeutics*. 7th ed. New York, NY: Macmillan Publishing Co Inc; 1985.
25. Gaffney GR, Berlin FS. Is there hypothalamic-pituitary-gonadal dysfunction in paedophilia? A pilot study. *Br J Psychiatry*. 1984;145:567–660.
26. Buhrich N, Theile H, Yaw A, Crawford A. Plasma testosterone, serum FSH and serum LH levels in transvestism. *Arch Sex Behav*. 1979;8:49–53.
27. Fox CA, Ismail AAA, Love DN, et al. Studies on the relationship between plasma testosterone levels and human sexual activity. *J Endocrinol*. 1972;52:51–58.
28. Rubin HB, Henson DE, Falvo RE, et al. The relationship between men's endogenous levels of testosterone and their penile responses to erotic stimuli. *Behav Res Ther*. 1979;17:305–312.
29. Purvis K, Landgren BM, Cekan Z, et al. Endocrine effects of masturbation in men. *J Endocrinol*. 1976;70:439–444.
30. Stearn EL, Winter JSD, Faiman C. Effects of coitus on gonadotropin, prolactin and sex steroids in man. *J Clin Endocrinol Metab*. 1973;37:687–691.
31. Rada RT, Laws DR, Kellner R. Plasma testosterone levels in the rapist. *Psychosom Med*. 1976;38:257–268.
32. Rada RT, Laws DR, Kellner R, Stivastava L, et al. Plasma androgens in violent and nonviolent sex offenders. *Bull Am Acad Psychiatry Law*. 1983;11:149–157.
33. Rada RT. Plasma androgens and the sex offenders. *Bull Am Acad Psychiatry Law*. 1980;8:456–464.
34. Berlin FS, Meinecke CF. Treatment of sex offenders with antiandrogenic medication: conceptualization, review of treatment modalities and preliminary findings. *Am J Psychiatry*. 1981;138:601–607.
35. Bradford JMW. Organic treatments for the male sexual offender. In: Prentky RA, Quinsey VL, eds. *Human Sexual Aggression: Current Perspectives. Annals of the New York Academy of Sciences*. Vol 528. New York, NY: The New York Academy of Sciences; 1988.
36. Cooper AJ. Progestogens in the treatment of male sex offenders: a review. *C J Psychiatry*. 1986;31:73–79.
37. Regenstein QR, Reich P. Pedophilia occurring after onset of cognitive impairment. *J Nerv Ment Dis*. 1978;166:794–798.
38. Cooper AJ. Medroxyprogesterone acetate (MPA) treatment of sexual acting out in men suffering from dementia. *J Clin Psychiatry*. 1987;48:368–370.
39. Hucker SJ, Ben-Aron MH. Elderly sex offenders. In: Langevin RL, ed. *Erotic Preferences, Gender Identity, and Aggression in Men: New Research Studies*. Hillsdale, NJ: Lawrence Erlbaum Associates Publishers; 1985.
40. Graber B, Hartmann K, Coffman JA, et al. Brain damage among mentally disoriented sex offenders. *J Forensic Sci*. 1982;27:125–134.
41. Scott ML, Cole JK, McKay SE, et al. Neuropsychological performance of sexual assaulters and pedophiles. *J Forensic Sci*. 1984;29:1114–1118.
42. Hendricks SE, Fitzpatrick DF, Hartmann K, et al. Brain structure and function in sexual molesters of children and adolescents. *J Clin Psychiatry*. 1988;49:108–112.
43. Blumer D. Changes of sexual behavior related to temporal lobe disorder in man. *J Sex Res*. 1970;6:173–180.
44. Kluver H, Bucy PE. Preliminary analysis of functions of the temporal lobes in monkeys. *AMA Arch Neurol Psychiatry*. 1939;42:979–1000.
45. Terzian H. Observations on the clinical symptomatology of bilateral partial or total

removal of the temporal lobes in man. In: Baldwin M, ed. *Temporal Lobe Epilepsy*. Springfield, Ill: Charles C Thomas; 1958.
46. Langevin R. Sexual anomalies and the brain. In: Marshall WL, Laws DR, Barbaree HE, eds. *Handbook of Sexual Assault: Issues, Theories, and Treatment of the Offender*. New York, NY: Plenum Press; 1990.
47. Blumer D. Hypersexual episodes in temporal lobe epilepsy. *Am J Psychiatry*. 1970;126:1099–1106.
48. Gastaut H, Collomb H. Étude du comportement sexuel chez les épileptiques psychomteurs. *Ann Mediopsychol*. 1954;112:657–696.
49. Davies BM, Morgenstern FS. A case of cysticercosis and temporal lobe epilepsy, and tranvestism. *J Neurol Neurosurg Psychiatry*. 1960;23:247–249.
50. Epstein AW. Relationship of fetishism and transvestism to brain and particularly to temporal lobe dysfunction. *J Nerv Dis*. 1961;133:247–253.
51. Kolarsky A, Freund K, Machek J, et al. Male sexual deviation: association with early temporal lobe damage. *Arch Gen Psychiatry*. 1967;17:735–743.
52. Taylor DC. Psychiatry and sociology in the understanding of epilepsy. In: Mandelbrote BM, Gelder MG eds. *Psychiatric Aspects of Medical Practice*. London, England: Staples; 1972.
53. Rada RT. Alcoholism and forcible rape. *Am J Psychiatry*. 1975;132:444–446.
54. Rada RT. Alcohol and rape. *Medical Aspects of Human Sexuality* 1975;9:48–60.
55. Rada RT, Kellner R, Laws DR, et al. Drinking, alcoholism and the mentally disordered sex offenders. *Bull Am Acad Psychiatry Law*. 1978;6:296–300.
56. Briddel DW, Rimm DC, Caddy GR, et al. Effects of alcohol and cognitive set on sexual arousal to deviant stimuli. *J Abnorm Psychol*. 1978;87:418–430.
57. Barbaree HE, Marshall WL, Yates E, et al. Alcohol intoxication and deviant sexual arousal in male social drinkers. *Behav Res Ther*. 1983;21:365–373.
58. Barbaree HE. Stimulus control of sexual arousal. In: Marshall WL, Laws DR, Barbaree HE, eds. *Handbook of Sexual Assaults: Issues, Theories, and Treatment of the Offender*. New York, NY: Plenum Press; 1990.
59. Langevin R, Ben-Aron MH, Coulthard R, et al. The effect of alcohol on penile erection. In: Langevin R, ed. *Erotic Preference, Gender Identity, and Aggression in Men: New Research Studies*. Hillsdale, NJ: Lawrence Erlbaum Associates Publishers; 1985.
60. Ward NG. Successful lithium treatment of transvestism associated with manic-depression. *J Nerv Ment Dis*. 1975;161:204–206.
61. Kafka MP. *Preliminary observations on a relationship between paraphilias and major affective disorders*. Presented at the 8th annual Research and Data Conference of the Association for the Behavioral Treatment of Sex Abusers; October 5–8, 1989; Seattle, Wash.
62. Kafka MP. Successful antidepressant treatment of nonparaphilic sexual addictions and paraphilias in men. *J Clin Psychiatry*. 1991;52:60–65.
63. Perilstein RD, Lipper S, Friedman LJ. Three cases of paraphilias responsive to fluoxetine treatment.*J Clin Psychiatry*. 1991;52:169–170.
64. Carnes P. *Out of the Shadows: Understanding Sexual Addiction*. Minneapolis, Minn: Comp Care Publishers; 1983.
65. Winslow JT, Insel TR. Neurobiology of obsessive compulsive disorder: a possible role for serotonin. *J Clin Psychiatry*. 1990;51:27–31.

5

Behavioral and Cognitive View on Sexual Perversion

Although there is a vast literature in the behavioral tradition on general principles of learning theory and the acquisition of behaviors, and a more recent emphasis on the role of cognitions in clinical disorders, there is a scarcity of integrated conceptualizations of these elements as related to the etiology and maintenance of sexual perversions. Unlike the psychodynamic orientations that have generated a variety of rich, if speculative, theories on the development of sexual perversions, the behavioral and more contemporary cognitive-behavioral integrations display a dearth of explanatory themes on sexual deviations, although they have made significant contributions to this field through their pragmatic treatment approaches.[1] In this chapter, we will review some of the basic behavioral and cognitive views on the formation of sexual perversion, and also attempt to articulate a more coherent view on the genesis of sexual deviation within the tradition of learning theory.

MODELS OF LEARNING BEHAVIOR

We envision a cognitive-behavioral perspective on perversion as one that would combine aspects of classical conditioning, instrumental or operant conditioning, and social learning factors, each of which are pervaded throughout by cognitively mediated processes, including conscious fantasy productions. A brief description of each of these approaches[2] will clarify the role they may play in an inclusive understanding of sexual perversion. In classical conditioning, which was discovered by Ivan Pavlov[3] in 1927, an unconditioned stimulus (UCS) such as food in a dog's mouth, elicits the unconditioned response (UCR) of salivation. If the salivation is repeatedly paired with a neutral stimulus such as the sound of a bell, the sound of the bell will become the conditional stimulus (CS) that elicits salivation, the conditional response (CR). Repeated pairings strengthen this response; lack of pairings weakens the response, leading to its extinction. The process of stimulus generalization may occur, in which the individual responds to stimuli similar to the CS as if it were the CS itself. Operant or instrumental conditioning, originally stemming from Thorndike's[4] Law of Effect, indicates that responses that result in satisfying consequences will be strengthened, while responses that lead to unsatisfying consequences are unlikely to be repeated. Building upon these observations, Skinner[5] has formulated the basic principles of learning to be related to reinforcement, or a positive consequence that increases the frequency of the behavior; and a punishment or a negative reinforcement that decreases the frequency of the behavior. Once established, an operantly conditioned response is maintained through reinforcement, and to a great extent the schedule of reinforcement (whether it occurs part-time, or is withheld in certain instances, is variable or fixed) controls the behavior. Social learning, as developed by Bandura,[6] postulates that change can take place by virtue of observational, imitative, or modeling phenomena. No particular reinforcement is needed to accomplish this learning. However, vicarious reinforcement and punishment may, in fact, take place because the individual is able to perceive the consequences of the model's behavior. During this social learning process, the individual forms mental schemata about the observed behavior, which may not replicate the observed behavior precisely, but are constructed strategies, outlooks, and rules that reflect the basic substance of the behavior. These schemata can then serve to influence the individual's feeling and actions.[7] Although earlier behavioralists, particularly in the classical and operant conditioning schools, did not sufficiently acknowledge the role of cognition, contemporary learning theorists fully appreciate the importance of cognitive processes in mediating between the stimulus and response.

Laws and Marshall[8] have delineated 10 fundamental principles derived from classical, operant, and social learning theory to explain the formation of deviant sexual preference and behavior. They cite Seligman's[9] concept of prepared learning in which the individual develops a repertoire of specific responses to specific stimuli and not to others as a means of developing sexual responses to normative heterosexual stimuli. Through a constellation of classical, operant, and social learning processes that are environmentally and adventitiously generated, highly deviant stimuli can be linked to sexual responsivity. Classical conditioning underscores the fact that the deviant sexual act becomes paired with a pleasurable response and then becomes habitually eroticized. This pleasurable bond can become internalized into a sexual fantasy, which is reinforced through masturbation.

In their study of 45 sexual deviants, McGuire et al[10] have found that sexual deviancy actually develops much more gradually than was formally thought in that the environment (sexual) stimulus, which may be traumatizing, only supplies a key fantasy for subsequent masturbation. Because the sexual incident is usually a real-life experience, the incident acts as a strong stimulus for masturbatory fantasy. This fantasy, stored in memory, also undergoes the normal psychological processes of recall, including distortion and selection of cues. Repeated masturbation to the fantasy continues to increase its stimulus value. Simultaneously, other sexual stimuli begin to lose their stimulus value and eventually are extinguished due to lack of reinforcement. Another important factor in the development of the sexual deviation found in more than half of the patients studied was their belief that they could not achieve a normal sex life. McGuire et al[10] believe that their findings have certain implications for the treatment of sexual deviants. "Since the original conditioning was carried out in most cases to fantasy alone, treatment also need only be to fantasy... patients can be warned of the conditioning effect of orgasms on the immediately preceding fantasy... the fantasy in the five seconds just before orgasm must be of normal sexual intercourse..." (p 187).

In regard to the behavioral enactment of the sexual fantasy, such an enactment can strengthen the habit potential of the sexual deviance if the operant consequences are reinforcing and, conversely, weaken the habit potential (and thus lead toward extinction) if the operant consequences are negative or punishing. For example, for the exhibitionist, a self-satisfying response from the victim, which is a positive operant consequence, would tend to reinforce the deviant behavior, while the exhibitionist who gets arrested, and thus experiences a negative or a punishing operant consequence, would tend to extinguish the behavior. Obviously, the issues of the consistency and/or the schedule of reinforcing and/or punishing operants plays a crucial role in the acquisition and maintenance of the deviant behavior. For instance, the exhibitionist may temporarily stop his sexual acting out after arrest, but further exhibitionistic acts may elicit enough pleasure to reinstitute the deviant behavior. In this entire acquisition process of deviant behavior, Laws and Marshall[8] note that "old Pavlovian associations are being re-paired, and new pairings are being introduced; old operants continue to be reinforced and new ones are created" (p 213). Hence, classical and operant conditioning processes work interactively.

Another integral feature in the formation of deviant behavior pointed out by Laws and Marshall[8] is the phenomenon called chaining of behavior. This process refers to the fact that habituated behavior is composed of "functionally linked sequences of instrumental acts... usually performed in serial order, each sequence triggering the next, culminating in some reinforcing activity" (p 217). Chains have particular significance in sexual deviance because it is often carried out in a ritualistic manner, so that each component reinforces the probability of its recurrence as well as initiates the action of the next component in the linkage leading up to the ultimate reinforcing phenomenon: orgasmic release. In addition to overt activity, chaining can also involve internal fantasy experiences. The use of sequential fantasy productions has particular importance in the crucial self-control, cognitive and behavioral task of covert sensitization, which will be discussed in detail in the treatment section of this book.

Social learning processes constitute the third major fact in the behavioral-oriented view on the formation of sexual deviance. Laws and Marshall[8] draw upon the works of Bandura,[6,11] and Bandura and Walters[12] in proposing three fundamental processes relevant to the learning of sexual behavior: (1) participant modeling (which involves the individual's observing and copying the behavior of a model); (2) vicarious learning (which involves nonparticipant observation of the behavior); and (3) symbolic modeling (which involves the use of mental imagery and fantasy). In these social learning experiences, the individual does not need to undergo direct reward or punishment to learn new behaviors. Novel responses can be acquired by modeling the actions of others, who themselves are being rewarded or punished. "Internal factors," as beliefs, expectations, imagery, and fantasies, are invariably involved in the individual's acquisition of new behaviors via modeling. Indeed, in his more recent works, Bandura[7] has emphasized the fact that the cognitive factors operate at all levels of learning: classical conditioning, operant conditioning, and social learning processes.

COGNITION AND BEHAVIOR

The so-called "cognitive revolution" has become an impetus for the acknowledgment of the significance of cognition in the development and subsequent treatment of dysfunctional behaviors. Cognitions may include belief systems, interpretations of events, attitudes, and self-perceptions, or representation. Historically, the cognitive revolution, as explicated by Gardner,[13] delineated such necessary key features of cognitive science as the varying levels of mental representation, the relevance of computer simulation and computation as models of human thought, and the "de-emphasis on affect, context, culture, and history" (p 41). According to Mahoney,[14] the most recent development in the evolving cognitive movement involves a more "constructivistic" sensibility that "rejects the computer analogy entirely and appeals to active (participatory) processes in knowing..." (p 79). "The single most distinctive feature of constructivism is the assertion that all cognitive phenomena—from perception and memory to problem solving and consciousness—entail active and proactive processes . . . the organism is an active participant in its own experiences as well as in learning" (p 100). This, in effect, reintroduces what Gardner[13] has dismissed, that is, "affect, context, culture, and history," as vital determinants in the shaping of experiences.

The acquisition of sexual behavior, including deviant sexual behavior, involves manifold cognitive factors which permeate the entire learning process. We suggest that these cognitive factors can best be understood by categorizing them as either "direct" or "indirect" cognitive influences. The most direct cognitive factor is the key fantasy production shaped by early learning experiences. As McGuire et al[10] have noted, the ideational-oriented fantasy material, which may stem from an actual traumatic experience, becomes, in effect, the building block of a subsequently conditioned sexual arousal pattern. Complicated learning processes sustain, elaborate, or modify this fantasy. This conscious fantasy material eventually takes on a meaningful life of its own. Indeed, fantasy is not simply a mechanical product of external events or stimuli, but it itself shapes and directs, and so "constructs," idiosyncratic patterns of sexual relating. However, as Protter and Travin[1] have pointed out, unlike the psychodynamic theorists who explore all topographical levels, namely the conscious, preconscious, and unconscious, and their developmental referents, behaviorists restrict themselves to understanding only the conscious level of fantasy production. The intensity of this conscious fantasy production can to a considerable extent be assessed by penile erection measurements with audio and visual stimulus cues. This assessment procedure may be considered an objective measure available for the individual's arousal pattern which, in effect, taps into the fantasy structure and quantifies the level of arousal in the paraphiliac.

A variety of indirect cognitive factors may facilitate deviant sexual behavior or, in effect, impede nondeviant, normative sexual behavior. Among these facilitating factors are attitudes and beliefs derived from sociocultural influences such as sexist attitudes toward women with themes of male dominance, acceptance of rape myths, violence-promoting cultures, and pornographic stimulation. These faulty attitudes and beliefs may become funneled into a personal belief system of cognitive distortions wherein the individual misperceives and misevaluates the consequences of his behavior for others. Murphy,[15] utilizing Bandura's[6] social learning theory, categorizes three major cognitive processes that enable the individual to suspend his normal self-evaluative behavior. These cognitive processed adapted from Bandura are (1) making reprehensible conduct socially and ethically acceptable, (2) misconstruing the consequences of the behavior, and (3) devaluing or attributing blame to the victim. Pedophilic behavior may thus be facilitated by a combination of learned cognitive constructs that reinforce the individual's propensity for deviant sexuality. These constructs may include the need for pronounced dominance over the weaker child victim, as well as the need to rationalize the behavior and minimize its effect, often by devaluing and attributing blame to the victim.

Among the cognitive distortions that may impede the development of normal heterosexual behavior are a variety of self-constructs which include beliefs, expectations, and self-labeling. If these self-constructs center around fear of failure with the opposite sex, particularly around a male's expectations of rejection by an adult female and feelings of worthlessness in relationship to women, this may contribute to an overall sense of male inadequacy and lack of assertiveness. Given these impediments to normative sexuality, the individual may be drawn toward aberrant sexual outlets.

DISCUSSION

The cognitive-behavioral views on sexual perversion, as we noted earlier, have made their most significant contribution in the areas of intervention and treatment. Etiologically, the core concept is the conditioned sexual fantasy that is paired by orgasmic reinforcement and subsequently elaborated by other learning principles. But, as Rosen and Beck[16] note, "conditioning processes are seldom viewed as a sufficient explanation for the acquisition of paraphiliac arousal," although they add that "both classical and instrumental conditioning procedures have been widely used in the application of behavioral approaches to treatment" (p 218).

Indeed, Earls and Quincey[17] have pointed out that there is no definitive scientific data linking sexual offenders with certain behavioral, attitudinal, or cognitive deficits. These authors conclude that "it is possible that we have already identified the only distinguishing characteristic of sexual offenders, i.e., their inappropriate sexual arousal ... " (p 380). It should be noted that the same kind of observations can be made about other hypothesized learning deficiencies attributed to the paraphiliac. Thus, as various empirical studies have indicated, such deficiencies as sex education and pornographic influences may be, in varying degrees, contributory to the maintenance of the sexual deception, but not etiologically related to it per se. For example, after reviewing the literature on the influences of pornography, Murrin and Laws[18] conclude that, whereas nonoffenders tend to reduce pornographic consumption in adolescence, sex offenders increase their use of pornography as they grow into adulthood.

In conclusion, learning and cognitive factors play a significant role in the etiology and maintenance of deviant sexual behavior, although the exact nature of this process has not been empirically delineated. Our view, which is pluralistic in nature, is that a cognitive-behavioral perspective is one important piece in the overall understanding of sexual deviance.

REFERENCES

1. Protter B, Travin S. Sexual fantasies in the treatment of paraphiliac disorders: a bimodal approach. *Psychiatr Q.* 1987;58:279–297.
2. Wortman CB, Loftus EF. *Psychology.* 3rd ed. New York, NY: Alfred A Knopf Inc; 1988.
3. Pavlov IP, Anrep GV, trans. *Conditioned Reflexes* London, England: Oxford University Press, 1927.
4. Thorndike EL. *The Fundamentals of Learning.* New York, NY: Teacher's College; 1932.
5. Skinner BF. *The Behavior of Organisms: An Experimental Analysis.* New York, NY: Appleton-Century-Crofts; 1938.
6. Bandura A. *Social Learning Theory.* Englewood Cliffs, NJ: Prentice-Hall; 1977.
7. Bandura A. *Social Foundation of Thought and Action: A Social Cognitive Theory.* Englewood Cliffs, NJ: Prentice-Hall; 1986.
8. Laws DR, Marshall WL. A conditioning theory of the etiology and maintenance of deviant sexual preference and behavior. In: Marshall WL, Laws DR, Barbaree HE,

eds. *Handbook of Sexual Assault: Issues, Theories and Treatment of the Offender.* New York, NY: Plenum Press; 1990.
9. Seligman MEP. Phobias and preparedness. *Behav Ther.* 1971;2:307–320.
10. McGuire RJ, Carlisle JM, Young BG. Sexual deviation as conditioned behavior: a hypothesis. *Behav Res Ther.* 1965;2:185–190.
11. Bandura A. *Aggression: A Social Learning Analysis.* Englewood Cliffs, NJ: Prentice-Hall; 1973.
12. Bandura A, Walters RH. *Social Learning and Personality Development.* New York, NY: Holt, Rinehart & Winston; 1963.
13. Gardner H. *The Mind's New Science: A History of the Cognitive Revolution.* New York, NY: Basic Books Inc; 1985.
14. Mahoney MJ. *Human Change Processes: The Scientific Foundations of Psychotherapy.* New York, NY: Basic Books Inc; 1991.
15. Murphy WD. Assessment and modification of cognitive distortions in sex offenders. In: Marshall WL, Laws DR, Barbaree HE, eds. *Handbook of Sexual Assault: Issues, Theories and Treatment of the Offender.* New York, NY: Plenum Press; 1990.
16. Rosen RC, Beck JG. *Patterns of Sexual Arousal.* New York, NY: Guilford Press; 1988.
17. Earles CM, Quinsey VL. What is to be done? Future research on the assessment and behavioral treatment of sex offenders. *Behav Sci Law.* 1985;3:377–390.
18. Murrin MR, Laws DR. The influence of pornography on sexual crime. In: Marshall WL, Laws DR, Barbaree HE, eds. *Handbook of Sexual Assault: Issues, Theories and Treatment of the Offender.* New York, NY: Plenum Press; 1990.

6

Psychodynamic Perspectives of Sexual Perversion

In general, psychodynamic conceptualizations of sexual perversions have mirrored the periodic revisions and the major developments in psychoanalytic views over the past century. These developments can be understood as a progression from the earliest psychoanalytic paradigms—drive or instinctual—to more contemporary concerns with object-relational, interpersonal, and self psychological theory. Whereas earlier psychoanalysts focused on the primary dynamics of the Oedipal complex and accompanying castration anxiety, recent theorists concentrate on preoedipal concerns centering on separation anxiety and associated factors, such as early gender role, the rudimentary formation of the self, the significance of specific early traumatogenic events, and attachment and relational motifs.

REVIEW OF PSYCHODYNAMIC FORMULATIONS

Classical and Revisionistic Views

Freud's[1] original view of psychopathology, the so-called seduction theory, which he expounded in 1895, placed the responsibility for psychic disorders on the sexually perverse father who, in seducing the future-to-be-neurotic (the hysteric at this point in psychoanalytic theory), fully becomes the toxic etiologic agent of neurotic psychopathology. This focus on the hysteric also launched Freud on his revolutionary discovery of the unconscious. The hysteric, according to Freud, splits off the sexually traumatogenic event and its associated affect, only to have it return in an alienated form in the language of symptom formation. Freud's[2] heralded theoretical switch in 1899, from believing in the reality of the seductive father to defining the event as a fantasy, set the stage for this more focused work on sexuality. In his classic work *Three Essays on the Theory of Sexuality*,[3] published in 1905, Freud asserted that it is not the externally acting, sexually perverse parent, but the internally lodged, somatopsychological sexual instinct itself that is implicated in psychological illness. In this paradigm, the sexual instinct, as expressed in its most primitive and component form, is polymorphously perverse in nature. It proceeds through childhood in the psychosexual stages, becoming maturely integrated and synthesized in the child's overcoming of castration anxiety and resolution of the Oedipal complex. The problematic progression of this developmental achievement may result in either neurosis or perversion. In Freud's[3] early writings on sexuality, neurosis is the negative of perversion, meaning that the neurotic's symptomatic language, inhibited by civilization's constraining influence on the developing mind, is that of the disguised pervert. Such neurosis is thus opposed to the actual pervert's more "real" primitive sexual language, that of a bestial pleasure-seeking organism, unchecked by the internalization of culture, and hence more truly representative of man's basic, infantile instinctual essence. Perversion, then, in this early but foundational view, is a kind of primitively fixated and acted-out concretization of sexual libido, which, when manifested in adult life, is a carryover from infancy that has not undergone any transformation into mature adult genital activity.

The result is a sexuality that is symptomatically acted out in its raw component forms, unlike the neurotic (for Freud, again, the classic example being the "hysteric"), in whom sexuality is a compromise formation displaced in symbolic, nonovertly sexual forms. In contrast to neurosis, the sexually perverse symptom becomes an imperative, insistently driven sexuality, deviant in aim and object (in its infantile, nonheterosexual regressed form). It is syntonic in its pleasure-producing drive and less deflected by symbolic compromises through the inhibiting features of ego and superego structures. Subsequent views of perversion, advanced by Freud[4] himself as well as by others[5,6,7] in the classical ego line of psychoanalysis, somewhat altered these notions. They emphasized the defensive aspects of perverse behavior, as well as the various possible fusions of aggression with the sexual drive. This constituted a more fully acknowledged, dual instinct theory of human nature. Although perversion was seen as a developmental fixation, it took on features of a kind of "impulsive neurosis." This means that the development of perversion began to be understood as a complicated psychological process that, rather than remaining a pure id impulse, undeflected by ego and superego, goes through the oedipal stage in a way characterized by Gillepsie[5] "like a light ray refracted" (p 397). At this stage, then, the ego, and to a lesser extent the superego, were believed to be actively involved in the formation of perversion by displacement, transformation, and rechanneling processes. The symptomatic perverse behavior was therefore conceptualized as being able to substitute for earlier component instincts that had become repressed. The perversion may thus function in a host of defensively related operations in the service of general neurotic formation, and in the shoring up of flaws in the development of a sense of reality. The manifest perverse symptom, then, could be viewed as being a displaced form of primitive, unconscious sexuality and aggressivity with myriad meanings and fantasies. Some remnant of the infantile experience is preserved in the perverse symptomatology and is a carrier of the unconscious infantile sexuality through the process of displacement.[6]

The core dynamic of perversion within the classical conceptualization, though, is castration anxiety. Inasmuch as the young male needs to negotiate successfully the anxieties associated with castration in his maturational development toward heterosexual identification with the father, the male gender is vulnerable (unlike the female, whose castration is not threatened but is a factor of life to be accepted) to regression or fixation to a more immature, perverse sexuality, deviant in aim, object, and zone. The adult perverse behavior generally represents restitutive and defensive attempts to deny the fear and associated anxieties of the castration threat. This may be focused on the denial of the difference between sexes since "penisless" females bring up the dreaded fear of castration. This unconscious fantasy of the "phallic women" often remains a core underlying feature in the perverse enactment.[8] Sexual perverse symptoms may, variously, entail the use of inanimate objects, genital displays, viewings, or painful enactments in order to achieve orgastic satisfaction. These perverse symptoms often include regressive and defensive forms of unconscious reassurances, undoings, atonements, or rectifications, stemming from earlier oedipal castration threats, guilt, or fears.

The meaning of sexuality within Freudian psychology was embedded within an endogenous drive model.[9] It was understood as constituting the motivational force of all relational and attachment phenomena in human nature. Sexuality within this Freudian paradigm emanated intraphysically, whereby universal fantasy-laden themata epigenetically expressed the oedipal drama. This system, however, did not sufficiently take into account environmental, exogenous factors, particularly those of an early preoedipal nature, in which the configuration of the child's primary relationship with the mother assumed crucial significance in the developing individual's sense of sexuality. Such meanings as the primitive "breast mother," early core gender formations of identity, and the matrix of archaic sexual experience as it impacts on oedipal developmental issues were not addressed. The actual nature of the interaction with the early caretaking mother was to assume greater significance within the views of later revisionistic writers in the Freudian tradition. As already noted, Freud himself has written about the traumatogenic, seductive parent before he made his historic transition to the universality of the child's oedipal fantasy life. But it was toward the increasingly recognized impact of the early preoedipal mother that clinical theory in perversion has eventually shifted. This focus on the etiologic impact of very early maternal caretaking was buttressed by observational studies in infant research.

In his numerous writings, Stoller[12,13,14] has underscored a revised view of gender development and its etiologic relationship to the formation of perversion. He has modified Freud's notions by postulating an earlier preoedipal stage in gender identity and development. Stoller,[12] drawing on the work of Greenson,[15] identifies a stage of "protofemininity" in both sexes preceding oedipal dynamics. This protofemininity is marked by a symbiotic merger with the mother. Unlike the female child, the male needs to disengage ("disidentify") from this primary female identificatory state in order to develop in the direction of masculinity, a process that is enhanced by the presence of a male figure with whom the boy can identify. If this necessary separation process goes awry, what follows is an unsure gender identity formation with a consequent vulnerability to the development of sexual perversion. The male's apparent or covert hostility toward women may thus be viewed as "males' need for constant vigilance against their unacceptable yearning to return to the merging in the symbiosis" (p 17). Ovesey and Person,[16] in their studies on gender identity and sexual psychopathology do not postulate a protofeminine state per se, but rather emphasize conflicting merger fantasies with the mother as defenses against issues of separation and identity that may lead to problems in gender identity and cross-gender behaviors. In his unitary theory of sexual perversion, Socarides[17] also delineates "faulty gender-defined self identity" as one vital linkage in the formation of perversion.

Stoller[13] suggests that sexually traumatizing caretaking on the part of the mother, likely reflecting her own sexual-gender conflicts, undermines the needed separation-disidentifying process that would otherwise lead to her son's healthy sexual and gender development. Consequently, this son could be vulnerable to develop sexually perverse symptomatology. Stoller[14] believes that this perverse symptomatology represents an erotic form of hatred, meaning the urge to harm the object—often the traumatogenic mother—who has wounded the male by having subverted his gender identity development. This "hostility in perversion takes form in a fantasy of revenge hidden in the actions that make up the perversion and serves to convert childhood trauma to adult triumph" (p 8). There is a complicated mix of trauma, hostility, risk, excitement, and revenge embedded within the perverse scenario. It is as if the perverse individual replays the original trauma to undo and achieve victory over it. This may be done by dehumanizing the sexual object in some manner. Men in particular are prone to develop sexual perversion because of the powerful need to separate themselves from the mother during this vulnerable period, for fear of being overengulfed by her and losing their sense of male gender. Socarides[17] noted that there is both a fear of merging with the preoedipal mother and an inability to separate from her; this dilemma is central to the sexual perverse condition. Influenced by Mahler[10] and Spitz,[11] Socarides underscores the etiologic significance of separation-individuation during the preoedipal phase of development, as well as inadequate psychological maturations at critical periods.

Other revisionistic writers[18,19,20] have described the various maladaptive and traumatic effects of the preoedipal mother. Chasseguet-Smirgel,[18] for example, suggests that the future pervert has an inappropriate, close seductive relationship with the mother, who excludes the father. The child retains the illusion that "with his pregenital sexuality, his immature and sterile penis, he is an adequate sexual partner for his mother and has nothing to envy in his father" (p 91). He then projects his narcissism onto his pregenital zones and part objects, and he idealizes them, remaining attached to a pregenital model. The child, in effect, disavows the genital identification with the father by managing to avoid the Oedipal complex in this precocious sexual attachment to the mother.

McDougall[19] coined the term "neosexuality" to connote that the child's "psychic labor" creates the perverse sexuality in order to help him come to terms with the unconscious erotic problems of both parents. The child's relationship to the parents was in a subtle fashion unduly sexualized by his enactments of the parents' unconscious erotic desires and conflicts. The mother's early impinging bodily communications to the child as well as unconscious reactions to her own sexual arousal evoke archaic body-image problems in the infant at a time when he is beginning to form what Lichtenstein[21] has described as sexual identity. The sexual deviant in adulthood has "created his neosexual erotic theater as a protective barrier against a damaged corporeal image and against the loss of the body representation as an entity and with it the loss of a cohesive sense of ego identity" (p 273). This neosexual construction represents both a defensive attempt to cope with castration threats and a protection against the loss of ego identity, primitive aggression, and violent impulses.[19]

Relational Schools

The more recent relational schools in psychoanalysis, which include object relational, interpersonal, and self psychological schools, have deemphasized the centrality of drive theory. They have more radically than the Freudian revisionists focused on the significance of sexuality as a channel through which more primary motivations such as the seeking of safety, security, and attachment operate. The achievement of these motivational factors takes on a primary dynamic not reducible to sexual organ pleasure. From the relational perspective, the individual is embedded in an interpersonal field with the other in which the central struggle concerns the establishment of the self and of one's sense of identity. It is the vicissitudes of the self's relational patterns with the other, as the self moves toward the achievement of the above-mentioned motivational goals, that shape the role of sexuality rather than the other way around. Another important feature of the relational school of psychodynamics is the emphasis on the real maladaptive environment in the early development of the infant or child's sexual life, as opposed to the earlier, Freudian emphasis on endogenous, fantasy-laden, unconscious derivatives. From the relational perspective, perversion may be indicative of an unconscious conflict and/or arrested relational problem that had become sexualized consciously. The underlying meaning of the perversion may stem from a host of early interpersonal and characterological difficulties. The perversion may thereby be a means of dealing with a separation, a disguised form of hostility, a reparation, or a compulsive reassurance about one's sense of insecurity, particularly as regards sexual or gender identity. Although writers in the revisionist strain of the Freudian tradition have incorporated many elements of the relational schools, those in the relational perspective such as Mitchell[22] give less credence to drive theory and its associated features.

In a specifically object relational perspective, Masud Khan[23] has written on the mother's intense but impersonal bodily care of her infant, which affects his sexual development. The mother does not relate to the son in a nurturant caring way but as a "thing-creation." The child in later life development is continually trying to repair this bodily damage by "a specialized use of his reparative drive, ie, [the drive] towards the self as an idolized internal object" (p 13). Addicted to these early sensations of maternal bodily care, the pervert is driven to revitalize the thwarted self, enlisting the other in his perverse ritual as a kind of transitional object. According to Winnicott,[24] transitional phenomena are situated between subjective reality (omnipotently created reality) and objective reality (seeing the other as he or she actually is, which is respectful of their "otherness"). Khan[23] suggests that the sexual pervert sees the sexual objects as a kind of transitional phenomenon. This amounts to experiencing the sexual object as a collage of "mental fantasy[ies] of partial and inadequate bodily experiences of maternal care" (p 135). He terms this collage a "collated internal object." The sexual object is enlisted in reviving the self: a pseudo-dreamlike intimacy and ecstatic state of illusory control is achieved in the pervert's rituals, but "there is no object relatedness hence no nourishment" (p 23), as his activities are essentially solitary and alienating in nature.

Mitchell,[22] drawing upon the work of Winnicott[24] and Fairbairn,[25] states that object-seeking and emotional attachment underlie the motivational force of sexual perversion. The attempt to engage sexual objects centers around the themes of searching for the inaccessible or unavailable other, accommodating or surrendering oneself to meeting the expectations of the other, or escaping from and rebelling against an impinging or a dominating other. These core themes harken back to the early developmental vicissitudes of attempting to connect to the inaccessible or unavailable mother, or accommodating to an impinging mother. Inasmuch as all object-seeking is complicated, variable, and elusive, Mitchell[22] states that many of these core themes are present in the spectrum of human sexual activity, but especially in sexual perversion, where underlying anxiety, need, and desperation are prominent in the self's attempt to engage the other. The pleasure in sexual perversion serves as a channel to reach the other and is often a dialectic of the visible and the secret, the available and the withheld, and the surface and the depth—these dialectical themes are representative of the self attempt to reach the unavailable, elusive figures from early development. The satisfaction in the perverse act may derive from the defiant overcoming of a powerful, controlling mother introject. In general, the counteridentificatory manic triumph over one's primary sense of object relatedness, pleasurably expressed in the "dirty," "freeing" aspects of sexuality, may, in effect, represent the expression of one's true self as opposed to a false self adaptation that had to accommodate to an impinging figure in the past. Ghent[26] has made a similar point that certain perversions such as masochism may represent a misfired means of genuinely connecting and relating to the other.

From the self psychological perspective, perversion emphasizes the meaning of the perverse act in the context of the development of a coherent sense of self. According to Kohut,[27] the infant/child's basic need in development is the availability at critical periods of an empathic and mirroring maternal caretaking object, which he terms self-object. Under favorable circumstances—that is, when such mothering occurs and is buttressed by the presence of a paternal "self-object," whom the child can idealize—the child can develop normal and integrative sexual patterns of behavior. If there is a breakdown in this critical self and self-object matrix of empathic and mirroring relationships, perversion may develop. This breakdown, in effect, results in a "disintegration product," which appears as a sexualized drive. The perversion is a manifestation of this drive and an attempt to repair and shore up the weakened, fragmented, and insecure self by merging with a substitutive self-object. In other words, the perverse act may anesthetize, soothe, or bolster the sense of self, or self-esteem, thereby reviving a deadened disintegrative or weakened self state. These disabling self states were originally generated by earlier interpersonal abandonments, misattunements, intrusions, and other troubling interactive patterns.

CONTEMPORARY PLURALISTIC OUTLOOK

Sexual perversion is clearly too complicated a phenomenon to be fully explained by any one psychodynamic viewpoint. This notion is consistent with the pluralistic sensibility that psychic phenomena are capable of being understood from different perspectives, and that psychodynamic theories themselves are continually evolving. The sexually deviant person can therefore only be understood in the light of his own individual psychic experience and background, which may not necessarily conform to any one discrete school of thought. Freudian notions, of course, illuminated the perverse sexual possibilities implicit in human nature and development. These notions with their emphasis on castration anxiety and gender formation in the oedipal development stage also focused on the specifically sexual vulnerability of the male child as it relates to perverse formation. But Freudian emphasis on pansexuality as the bedrock of human nature and character formation, underemphasized the significance of interaction and relational factors, specifically, early maternal caretaking. It should be noted, though, that the Freudian tradition's focus on sexuality (and such factors as the primacy of the penis) still has relevance to our understanding of sexually perverse disorders. Despite the contemporary post-Freudian emphasis on preoedipal determinants of sexual perversion, some perverse behavior may lend itself better to explication by more classic oedipal dynamics, or by varying mixtures of the two. Furthermore, as Mitchell[28] points out, the attempt to confine issues in the development of self and object relationship to the preoedipal developmental time span is somewhat arbitrary, as the development of identity and the capacity for object relationship is an ongoing, lifetime process. Generally, some authors[17,29] have described individuals with sexual perversions of oedipal derivation as characteristically having more intact reality testing, self-concept, and ego boundaries than those individuals with sexual perversions stemming from preoedipal roots. This is understandable in that preoedipal issues deal with the most primary development processes in the formation of the self, distinctions between the self and others, and the foundation of a secure sense of identity that precedes triangular conflicts between mother, father, and child in the Oedipal complex.

Along these lines, Socarides[17] has outlined perversions within a classificatory system as (1) preoedipal (Type I and Type II), (2) oedipal, and (3) schizoperversion. According to Socarides, preoedipal perversions are those fixated in the preoedipal stage of development. The perversion rises from significant anxiety and is marked by an obligatory, inflexible pattern. There is an accompanying "gender-defended self identity disturbance" (p 73). The perverse act is needed "in order to insure ego survival and transiently stabilize the sense of self" (p 74). In the milder Type I preoedipal perversion, the Oedipal complex obscures other underlying preoedipal conflicts. In the more severe Type II preoedipal perversion, regression may lead to serious impairment of object relations and other ego functions. Usually, the Type II preoedipal perversion is associated with a narcissistic personality disorder of varying severity. The oedipal form of perversion results from a failure to resolve the Oedipal complex and from castration fears; this form of perversion is less involved in the basic function of keeping the sense of self intact. Schizoperversion involves individuals who are fixated in the symbiotic phase of early development. These individuals are psychotically disturbed; for them, the perverse acts represent a defense against dissolution of ego boundaries. Socarides emphasizes that oedipal conflicts may defend against the emergence of underlying preoedipal material, and vice versa, with an ongoing interplay between the two. This attempt to chronologize perverse psychopathology along a developmental time span can be heuristically helpful. However, as we noted above, Mitchell views the development of the self and object relationships, including their likely impact on perverse behavior, as a process that proceeds throughout the individual's lifetime, and thus cannot be confined solely to early "preoedipal" periods.

BRIEF COMMENTS ON SPECIFIC PERVERSIONS

Some of the more common psychodynamic themes specific to the sexual perversions will now be discussed briefly. Gabbard[29] has reviewed psychodynamic formulations of some of the specific sexual perversions. Exhibitionism can be understood from Fenichel's[7] early classical notions as the sexual pervert's need to expose his genitals to reassure himself against castration anxiety, and voyeurism as a fixation in the primal scene of parental sexual intercourse. Stoller[14] views the exhibitionist as an individual who needs to avenge his humiliation at the hands of women as a means to regain his sense of maleness. Mitchell[22] conceptualizes the exhibitionist's act as a sexualization of his profound need to be noticed.

The early Freudians described fetishism as originating from castration anxiety and the fetishistic article (such as a shoe or a woman's undergarment) as representing the "female penis"; while Greenacre,[31] in a revisionistic framework, understands the fetish as a kind of transitional object serving to reassure the individual's concerns about genital integrity. Kohut[27] states that the fetish serves as a replacement for the unavailable selfobject, while Mitchell sees the fetishistic article as an indication of the severe anxiety experienced with the loss of one's sense of self. Turning to transvestism, or heterosexual cross-dressing, Fenichel[7] sees the male child as overcoming his castration anxiety by fantasizing that his mother possesses a penis, and that cross-dressing signifies an identification with the phallic mother, while object relation theorists view cross-dressing as a kind of psychic maternal object. The classical view of pedophilia suggests that pedophilia signifies a narcissistic object choice in which the individual achieves the status of being the loved child (and, conversely, of being the loving mother), while the revisionistic Socarides[17] sees the pedophiliac patient as symbolically warding off engulfment from his mother and trying to eradicate his unconscious feminine identification. Ganzarin and Buchele[32] view incestuous pedophilics as attempting to elicit compassionate care from their own children by presenting themselves to them as victims.

Howells[33] has cited some psychodynamic considerations specific to pedophilia that are found in the literature. He includes Storr's[34] description of the pedophile's problem as stemming from a "sense of inferiority and related need for dominance" (p 59), Bell and Hall's[35] description of a pedophilic patient's interest in children as "an expression of the client's personal child-like level of functioning" (p 60); Fraser's[36] conceptualization of pedophilia as "the process of narcisstic inversion" (p 61); Kraemer's[37] belief that the pedophile is forever yearning for an idealized childhood; and Lambert's[39] focus on "hostile themes in pedophilic fantasy" (p 62).

Glick and Meyers[40] have comprehensively reviewed psychoanalytic conceptualizations of masochism. Earlier notions of Freud[41] centered on instinctual-based views, wherein masochism was understood as an inversion of a more primary aggressive drive redirected toward the self. The masochist achieves pleasure by identifying with the sadist. Later Freud[4] emphasized the role of unconscious guilt (as a result of oedipal wishes) wherein pain becomes a precondition for sexual pleasure. Fenichel[7] has written that masochistic patients appear to be accepting a "lesser evil"—that is, lesser than the fear of castration." Later post-Freudian views deemphasized the instinctual basis of masochism and stressed the role of object relations and the self. Reich[42] emphasized that the masochist coerces love and evokes guilt from the love object by means of his suffering, thereby indirectly expressing aggression. Elaborating on this theme, Reik[43] referred to the masochistic play as a "victory through defeat" (p 10). Brenman[44] stressed the role of projective mechanisms, particularly those of hostility. Berliner[45] more clearly delineated the masochist's replication of a hurtful and disturbed object relationship of the past. The masochistic scenario is an "adaptive response to a cruel or harsh external reality, the result of a traumatic environment. Libidinization of suffering was an attempt to maintain the love of the object who caused the suffering ... an attempt to deny the sadism through repression and turn unloving ill treatment into love ... the introjections of the object's sadism into the superego" (p 12). Valenstein,[46] in the same vein, conceptualizes that the attachment to pain stems from the painful affective tie characteristic of the early tie to the object. Consequently, giving up the painful affect is tantamount to giving up part of the self. Menaker,[47] who has emphasized the masochist's fears of fusion and loss of ego identity, anticipates the self psychological view as expressed by Stolorow.[48] Stolorow focuses on the narcissistic function of masochism. The masochistic tie to the sexual object is based on the need to restore and maintain a crumbling self representation by omnipotently executing "control over or identification with an idealized parental imago or through the reparative activation of the grandiose self" (p 14).

BRIEF NOTE ON INCEST

It is important to note that, although there are similarities between extrafamilial pedophilia and intrafamilial pedophilia (ie, incest), there are also important differences. As Groth[49] has pointed out, the psychodynamics of parent–child incest necessarily involve some form of family dysfunction. Hence, the interrelationships among the family members and the structure of the family network need to be investigated.

The family dynamics believed to contribute to the development of father–daughter incestuous behavior include certain notable themes. Kaufman et al[50] stress the fear of desertion among all family members as one such dynamic, since the family's reaction to this fear can lead to incestuous acting out. The family pattern often consists of a maternal grandmother who, having been deserted by her husband, selects a daughter resembling him in order to displace hostile feelings onto her. This daughter not only marries a man similar to her own father, a man who periodically deserts her, but also singles out a daughter to whom she can give up her responsibilities so as to create a role reversal, and she displaces the original hostility she felt for her mother onto this daughter. The need for a mother figure seems to be extremely important in members of this kind of family, and the incestuous behavior somehow serves on an unconscious level to reduce the level of anxiety about desertion. Lustig et al[51] postulate another important dynamic pertaining to incest. They point out that incestuous behavior serves as a tension-reducing defense in the dysfunctional family—a defense that works to maintain the integrity of the family unit. These authors list five factors necessary for father–daughter incest to occur: (1) the daughter replaces the mother's role, (2) the parents discontinue having sex with each other, (3) the father does not seek sex outside the family, (4) the family fears desertion and disintegration, and (5) the mother gives conscious or unconscious consent. Finally, Alexander[52] offers a systems theory approach to incest, maintaining that such behavior can occur within a closed family structure "characterized by decreased interaction with the environment, by minimal elaboration of functions and roles, and by an emphasis on homeostasis to the detriment of morphogenesis" (p 87).

FANTASY AND SEXUAL PERVERSION

Another seminal theme in the psychoanalytic understanding of perversion is the crucial role of fantasy. Historically, psychoanalysis, more than any other discourse, has emphasized the significance of fantasy in the etiology and maintenance of human sexual behavior. Indeed, the very definition of perversion necessarily includes fantasy-laden direction and meaning elaborated in the human mind, which may culminate in perverse activity.

Freud launched the psychodynamic understanding of fantasy by expanding the concept to embrace both unconscious and preconscious aspects. However, Laplanche and Pontalis[53] have commented that Freud did not clearly distinguish the levels in which fantasy is operative, namely the conscious, preconscious, and unconscious. They suggest that Freud was less interested in "establishing such a differentiation than in emphasizing the links between these different aspects" (p 316). Isaacs[54] has written that "the term fantasy has been used in varying senses and different times and by different authors" (p 73). She distinguishes between the use of "fantasy" and the alternative spelling of the term, "phantasy." The former, ie, fantasy, represents such things as conscious daydreams, reveries, etc, which in the Freudian tradition are representative of the earliest impulses of desire and of aggressiveness. Phantasy, on the other hand, applies to the "primary content of unconscious mental processes" (p 81). The unconscious fantasy, according to Beres,[55] is characterized by four features: unconsciousness, occurrence in childhood, wishfulfillment, and mental representation.

In the classical Freudian tradition, as well as in some early objects relations schools, particularly the school represented by Melanie Klein,[56] the term "unconscious fantasy" was tied to the notion of an instinctually based, "drive-structure" metapsychology.[9] This conceptualization of unconscious fantasy consisted of endogenous, universal, mental schemata that were invariably derived from early somatopsychical sexual and aggressive drive phenomena. Freud believed that these universal fantasies began in the oedipal phase of development, whereas Klein[57] and her co-workers[58] hypothesized that well-formed, endogenous fantasy material starts at an earlier preoedipal stage.

More recent psychoanalytic theories, as in the relational school direction, downplay the constitutive role of drive, and emphasize instead the mediating role of environmental factors in the formation of self and identity and the enduring importance of human attachment, relatedness, and intimacy. Hence, the actual environmental impact of such crucial experiences as early parental mothering and caretaking (or the lack thereof) provides the developmental precursors for the consolidation of the sense of self and vital attachment issues. The idiosyncratic meanings that the individual ascribes throughout these developmental processes are encapsulated in enduring fantasy themata that operate on all the typographical levels—conscious, preconscious, and unconscious. In this expanded framework, fantasy is thus not relegated to a narrow drive and defense conflict, but may represent conflictual matters in the self and relational spheres such as, for example, the conflict between separation-individuation versus merging with the maternal introject. The implication for sexual perversion is that conscious perverse fantasies, which are essential features in the perverse strategy, have representational meaning that psychically relates to these more expanded (not merely drive) preconscious and unconscious domains.

CONCLUSION

Although psychoanalysis had seemed to many to have reached a standstill in its understanding of sexual perversion, contemporary approaches have radically increased our understanding of the phenonmenon. For many years, such formulations as castration anxiety and its accompanying oedipal dynamics were perfunctorily applied to virtually all sexually perverse behavior. This has led to a sense of incredulity, if not antagonism, in those mental health professionals who are not necessarily psychoanalytically oriented. Indeed, the perception that psychoanalysis explains in a stereo-typical manner according to a universal formula all perverse symptoms, still exists in some quarters. It was the purpose of this chapter to illuminate a more pluralistic psychodynamic perspective, one that underlines the richness as well as uniqueness of the meanings of sexually perverse behaviors for the individual, particularly as these meanings are reflected in the individual's fantasy life.

REFERENCES

1. Breuer J, Freud S. *Studies on Hysteria.* Standard Edition. Vol 2. London, England: Hogarth Press; 1895.
2. Freud S. *Screen Memories.* Standard Edition. Vol 3. London, England: Hogarth Press; 1962; 299–322.
3. Freud S. *Three Essays on the Theory of Sexuality.* Standard Edition. Vol 7. London, England: Hogarth Press; 1905; 123–245.
4. Freud S. A child is being beaten. A contribution to the study of the origin of sexual perversions. In: *Collected Papers.* London, England: Hogarth Press; 1919;2:172–201.
5. Gillepsie WH. The general theory of sexual perversion. *Int J Psycho-anal.* 1956;37:396–403.
6. Sachs H, Goldberg RB, trans. On the genesis of perversions. *Psychoanal Q.* 1985;55:477–488.
7. Fenichel O. *The Psychoanalytic Theory of Neurosis.* New York, NY: Norton; 1945.
8. Bak RC. The phallic woman: the ubiquitous fantasy in perversions. *Psychoanal Study Child.* 1968;23:15–36.
9. Greenberg J, Mitchell S. *Object Relations in Psychoanalysis.* Boston, Mass: Harvard University Press; 1986.
10. Mahler MS. *On Human Symbiosis and the Vicissitudes of Individuation.* New York, NY: International Universities Press; 1968.
11. Spitz RA. *The First Year of Life.* New York, NY: International Universities Press; 1965.
12. Stoller RJ. *Presentation of Gender.* New Haven, Conn: Yale University Press; 1985.
13. Stoller RJ. *Perversion: The Erotic Form of Hatred.* New York, NY: Pantheon; 1975.
14. Stoller RJ. *Observing the Erotic Imagination.* New Haven, Conn: Yale University Press; 1985.
15. Greenson R. Disidentifying from mother: its special importance for the boy. *Int J Psychoanal.* 1968;49:370–374.
16. Ovesey L, Person E. Gender identity and sexual psychopathology in men: a psychodynamic analysis of homosexuality, transsexualism and transvestism. *J Am Acad Psychoanal.* 1973;1:53–72.
17. Socarides C. *The Preoedipal Origin and Psychoanalytic Therapy of Sexual Perversion.* Madison, Ct: International Universities Press; 1988.
18. Chasseguet-Smirgel J. *Creativity and Perversion.* Madison, Ct: International Universities Press; 1986.
19. McDougall J. *Theaters of the Mind: Illusion and Truth on the Psychoanalytic Stage.* New York, NY: Basic Books; 1985.
20. Greenacre P. Perversions: general considerations regarding their genetical and dynamic background. *Psychoanal Study Child.* 1960;23:47–62.

21. Lichtenstein H. Identity and sexuality: a study of their interrelationship in man. *J Amer Psychoanal Assoc.* 1961;9:179–260.
22. Mitchell SA. *Relational Concepts in Psychoanalysis: An Integration.* Cambridge, Mass: Harvard University Press; 1988.
23. Khan MMR. *Alienation in Perversions.* New York, NY: International Universities Press; 1979.
24. Winnicott DW. *The Maturational Process and Facilitating Environment.* New York, NY: International Universities Press; 1965.
25. Fairbairn WRD. *An Object-Relations Theory of the Personality.* New York, NY: Basic Books; 1952.
26. Ghent E. Masochism, submission, surrender. *Contemp Psychoanal.* 1990;26:108–136.
27. Kohut H. *The Restoration of the Self.* New York, NY: International Universities Press; 1971.
28. Mitchell SA. Object relations and the developmental tilt. *Contemp Psychoanal.* 1984;20:473–499.
29. Gabbard G. *Psychodynamic Psychiatry in Clinical Practice.* Washington, DC: American Psychiatric Press Inc; 1990.
30. Stolorow RD, Atwood GE, Brandchaft B. Masochism and its treatment. *Bull Menninger Clin.* 1988;52:504–509.
31. Greenacre P. The transitional object and the fetish: with special reference to the role of illusion. *Int J Psychoanal* 1970;51:447–456.
32. Ganzarin R, Buchele BJ. Incest perpetrators in group therapy: a psychodynamic perspective. *Bull Menniger Clin.* 1990;54:295–310.
33. Howells K. Adult sexual interest in children: considerations relevant to theories of aetiology. In: Cook N, Howells K, eds. *Adult Sexual Interest in Children.* New York, NY: Academic Press; 1981.
34. Storr A. *Sexual Deviation.* Hammondsworth: Penguin; 1964.
35. Bell AP, Hall CS. The personality of a child molester. In: Weinberg MS, ed. *Sex Research: Studies from the Kinsey Institute.* New York, NY: Oxford University Press, 1976.
36. Fraser M. *The Death of Narcissus.* London, England: Secker & Warburg; 1976.
37. Kraemer W. *The Forbidden Love: The Normal and Abnormal Love of Children.* London, England: Sheldon Press; 1976.
38. Gordon R. Paedophilia: normal and abnormal. In: Kraemer W, ed. *The Forbidden Love of Children: The Normal and Abnormal Love of Children.* London, England: Sheldon Press; 1976.
39. Lambert K. The scope and dimensions of paedophilias. In: Kraemer W, ed. *The Forbidden Love: The Normal and Abnormal Love of Children.* London, England: Sheldon Press; 1976.
40. Glick RA, Meyers DI, eds. *Masochism: Current Psychoanalytic Perspectives.* Hillsdale, NJ: The Analytic Press; 1988.
41. Freud S. (1915). *Instincts and Their Vicissitudes.* Standard Edition. London, England: Hogarth Press; 1957;14:117–140.
42. Reich W. *Character Analysis.* New York, NY: Orgone Institute Press; 1933.
43. Reik T. *Masochism and Modern Man.* New York, NY: Farrar & Rinehart; 1941.
44. Brenman M. On teasing and being teased and the problem of moral masochism. *Psychoanal Study Child.* 1952;8:264–285. New York, NY: International Universities Press.

45. Berliner B. The role of object relations in moral masochism. *Psychoanal Q.* 1958;27:38–56.
46. Valenstein A. On attachment to painful feelings and the negative therapeutic reaction. *Psychoanal Study Child.* 1973;28:305–392. New Haven, Conn: Yale University Press.
47. Menaker E. Masochism—a defense reaction of the ego. *Psychoanal Q.* 1953;22:205–225.
48. Stolorow RD. The narcissistic function of masochism (and sadism). *Int J Psychoanal.* 1975;56:441–448.
49. Groth AN. Patterns of sexual assault against children and adolescents. In: Burgess AW, Groth AN, Holmstrom LL, Sgroi SM, eds. *Sexual Assault of Children and Adolescents.* Lexington, Mass. Lexington Books; 1978.
50. Kaufman I, Peck AL, Tagiuri CK. The family constellation and overt incestuous relations between father and daughter. *Am J Orthopsychiatry.* 1954;24:266–279.
51. Lustig N, Dresser JW, Spellman SW, Murray TB. Incest: a family group survival pattern. *Arch Gen Psychiatry.* 1966;14:31–40.
52. Alexander PC. A systems theory of incest. *Fam Proc.* 1985;24:79–88.
53. Laplanche J, Pontalis JB. *The Language of Psycho-Analysis.* New York, NY: WW Norton & Co. 1973, 314–319.
54. Isaacs S. The nature and function of phantasy. *Int J Psychoanal.* 1948;XXIX:73–97.
55. Beres D. The unconscious fantasy. *Psychoanal Q.* 1962;31:309–328.
56. Klein M. *Envy and Gratitude.* London, England: Tavistock, Basic Books; 1957.
57. Klein M. Love, guilt and reparation. In: *Love, Hate and Reparation.* London, England: Hogarth Press; 1937.
58. Segal H. *Introduction to the Work of Melanie Klein.* New York, NY: Basic Books Inc, 1964.

7

The Assessment of Sexual Perversion

The clinical manifestation of sexually perverse behavior is extraordinarily diverse in its severity and form. The clinician may be confronted with a continuum of perversion or perverselike behaviors, ranging from relatively minor and transient fantasy-laden material to dangerous sexual acting out of a paraphiliac disorder. Cases in which sexual perversion may surface as a problem are seen in a whole host of different settings, treatment contexts, and referral networks. At one end of the spectrum, sexually perverse experiences may be disclosed in the course of ongoing psychoanalytic psychotherapy, perhaps even after several years of treatment. It is probably the case that most patients who undergo traditional psychotherapy and eventually reveal sexually perverse difficulties or experiences, originally came to treatment for a variety of nonsexual problems, eg, anxiety, depression, low self-esteem, and interpersonal difficulties. At the other end of the spectrum are convicted sex offenders, referred by criminal justice agencies, such as probation or parole. These convicted sex offenders often deny, minimize, and attempt to deceive the clinician about their involvement in unlawful sexuality.

Assessment of these cases for ultimate treatment recommendations depends largely on where they lie in this continuum. The issues are often ambiguous as to precisely what kind of assessment is most appropriate for the individual case. These assessments are relevant not only for clinical purposes, but may also have profound legal implications. Despite the fact that there is no uniformly accepted protocol for the evaluation of sexually deviant behaviors, we will discuss the assessment techniques that are commonly utilized. The use of any one of these techniques may vary with the nature and circumstances of the individual case. Obviously, those cases referred to the specialist for a paraphiliac disorder per se, as opposed to reports of deviant sexuality, which surface during the course of traditional psychotherapy, may require different utilization of the evaluative techniques suggested below.

COMPREHENSIVE PSYCHIATRIC INTERVIEW

The standard comprehensive psychiatric interview typically includes the chief complaint, history of present illness, past psychiatric and psychosocial histories, mental status examination, and diagnostic impression. In evaluating a paraphiliac individual, the cardinal concern is identifying what other psychopathology may coexist with, or indeed be contributory to, the deviant sexuality. Major concerns include the presence of a psychosis, organic impairment or disorder, mental retardation, alcohol and/or substance abuse, and the presence of a severe personality disorder, with particular emphasis on antisocial and borderline features. Other important clinical concerns include coexisting depression with anxiety, and compulsions such as gambling, eating disorders, and general sexual compulsivity. It is important to ascertain the presence of these accompanying conditions, because they may preclude involvement in a particular form of treatment, and may merit referral for treatment of the coexisting problem prior to, or in place of, the sexual symptomatology. These conditions include psychosis, organic impairment or disorder, mental retardation, alcohol and/or substance abuse, severe personality disorder, and compulsive and addictive disorders. It is estimated that at most 5% of persons who present with sexually deviant symptomology suffer from major psychotic disorders such as schizophrenia or manic psychosis.[1] Targeting the underlying psychosis as presumptively contributing to the deviant sexual acting out, the treatment of choice would entail psychotropic medication. A small number of cases have been reported where the perverse sexual behavior began after the individual had developed organic brain deficits subsequent to a stroke or a brain tumor. Additionally, there are reports suggesting a possible relationship in some individuals between disorders such as Klinefelter's syndrome or temporal lobe epilepsy, and deviant sexuality.[2] Obviously, these conditions merit a thorough medical and neurological workup. Inasmuch as mentally retarded adults function at emotionally and developmentally much younger ages, some of these individuals are prone to sexual interaction with small children. Obviously, mentally retarded individuals can develop any other paraphiliac disorder. These individuals can be treated with specialized treatment techniques.[3]

In cases in which alcohol and/or substance abuse are present, an assessment needs to be made of the extent of alcohol or substance abuse, with emphasis placed on whether this abuse is chronic or only occurs during the commission of the sexual act, thereby serving as a disinhibiting factor or, later on, as a rationalization by the individual for the act itself.[4] Estimates of the incidence of alcohol and/or substance abuse, both in regard to chronicity and solely at the time of the sexual act itself, are substantial.[5] If there is an alcohol or drug problem, we recommend that these individuals get treatment for this in addition to specialized treatment for the paraphilia. In serious cases of alcohol or substance abuse, we insist that the patients get their drug problem under control by enrolling in an appropriate treatment program prior to treatment for the sexual disorder. It needs to be emphasized that an individual who continues to drink or abuse drugs has difficulty in controlling sexual urges.

Obviously, individuals with paraphiliac disorders may manifest a whole range of characterological problems[6] (as do other patients with primary DSM-III-R, Axis-I diagnoses), but what specifically needs to be investigated in these cases with personality disorders is the presence of severe antisocial and borderline features. Antisocial individuals often display dishonesty, exploitativeness, manipulativeness, and considerable lack of empathy and concern for others. Hence, antisocial individuals are exceedingly difficult to engage in treatment because of their deceitfulness. Furthermore, these individuals often show a complete lack of remorse about their victimizing others, even if the victimization was tinged with cruelty and violence. The prognosis for the successful treatment of these antisocial individuals is poor. Borderline individuals, who can be characterized as having features of psychic instability with vulnerability to episodes of decompensation and poor reality testing, often prove to be a significant challenge to engage in specialized sexual treatment programs. These patients have difficulties with limit setting and forming reliable therapeutic alliances. Often their paraphiliac symptomatology is accompanied by unstable and impulsive sexual acting out of a polymorphous perverse nature.[7] Although the prognosis for this kind of patient is somewhat better than that of the antisocial type, both of these severe personality-disordered conditions require enormous investments of time and energy—investments frequently beyond the resources of any one treatment setting.

The relationship of depression with anxiety disorders to sexual disorders needs careful examination, as it is not uncommon for individuals to become severely depressed and/or anxious following discovery or arrest as a result of the unlawful sexual act. Events such as the breakup of the family, the loss of job, the humiliation in the community, and the loss of self-esteem may precipitate severe depression with suicidal preoccupation. In less severe cases of depression, the patient will have to be treated either before or in addition to the specialized sexual therapy.[8] Finally, it has been increasingly common in our experience to find paraphiliac-disordered individuals suffering from "cross" addictions such as gambling, eating disorders, and general sexual compulsivity. It is prudent in some cases to refer these individuals to other specialized programs that treat these disorders.

DETAILED SEXUAL INTERVIEW

A major area of psychiatric inquiry that the clinician commonly avoids is the obtaining of a detailed sexual history from the patient. Obviously, in regard to the sexually perverse patient, a detailed sexual interview is absolutely necessary in order to understand the nature of the disorder. Even when this kind of patient is referred for treatment, the clinician may show a hesitancy to inquire directly into this area; this hesitancy, at times, may reflect the therapist's own sexual anxiety and discomfort. The choice of the most prudent way to approach this area depends on the context and circumstances in which the sexual problem presents itself, eg, as the referred problem, or in the course of therapy for some other presenting problem. If the patient is specifically referred for treatment of a deviant sexual disorder, the therapist should take a direct, matter-of-fact, and nonjudgmental approach to this area of functioning, as with any other class of behaviors. If in the course of ongoing psychotherapy the patient discloses that he has engaged in sexually perverse behavior such as lewdly exhibiting himself on different occasions over a period of time, the therapist may more tactfully draw from aspects of the two chief components of the detailed sexual interview—the sexual history and the deviant sexual pattern. In the sexual history, inquiry is focused on the historical antecedents of the sexual perversion. It is important to elicit the patient's earliest sexual awakenings, sexual play as a child, traumatogenic incidents such as the patient's personal molestation, sexual fantasies with onset and frequency of accompanying masturbation, nocturnal emissions, pattern of normative sexuality, including dating, petting foreplay, sexual intercourse, and description of any sexual anxiety or dysfunction.

It is important to ascertain the tone and sexual atmosphere in the home environment. This should include parental attitudes and moralistic views toward sexuality, as well as parental modeling of sexual activity in their own lives and as a marital couple. Factors such as proper generational boundaries demarcating children from adults, the tolerance of family members' exhibiting their nakedness, the presence of pornographic material, the nature of demonstrative affection displayed between parents, and the extent of sibling sexual interplay should be included. It should be pointed out that retrospective accounts of familial sexuality have become an extremely controversial area, particularly in regard to what constitutes sexual abuse. But if the patient reports that he experienced a peculiar, uncomfortable feeling with a parent's physical closeness, this description should be accepted and explored. Although some reports of incest may indeed be exaggerated or distorted, the prudent course for the clinician is to integrate this material with the entire clinical picture.

Regarding the deviant sexual pattern, the clinician needs to elicit a complete history of the deviant sexual activity from the patient. In cases where the patient is involved with third-party agencies such as the criminal justice system or family court, corroborating reports should be obtained. Questions must be directed so as to obtain detailed descriptions of the onset of deviant fantasies, their frequency and duration, and how they are incorporated into masturbatory activity. Typically, these deviant fantasies begin during adolescence, but there is considerable variability as to age of onset. Although clinical observation has indicated that even so-called normal heterosexuals sometimes have deviant fantasies, the form and content of these kinds of fantasies are of the utmost importance in paraphiliacs. The elements that define fantasy production from the more normative to the deviant are the degree of compulsivity, preoccupation, and accompanying distress. We need to remember that many of the more severe sexual deviates such as pedophiles and sexual sadists initially are reluctant to disclose the extent of their deviant fantasies.[9] The reason for this is that acknowledgment of these fantasies would more compellingly break through their distortion and denial pattern, and hence force them to take responsibility for the nature of their paraphiliac disorders.

It is also crucial to determine the onset of the actual deviant sexual behavior and its subsequent enactments. The onset of deviant behavior is believed to occur some time after the beginning of deviant fantasies; this time period, though, varies widely. It is vital to understand the internal subjective factors as well as the external circumstances that were operative during the initial deviant sexual act and the subsequent behavioral pattern. This line of inquiry, in effect, is directed toward the larger question of why and how conscious sexual fantasies become transformed by a chain of circumstances into deviant sexual acts. We must emphasize that what we are attempting to delineate is an offense pattern that is unique for each individual offender. Often integral to the pattern are accompanying cognitive distortions.[10] These are a series of rationalizations, misconstruings, and faulty thinking that serve to justify and excuse, and thereby to perpetuate the activity. For example, an incest perpetrator might rationalize that having sex with his 8-year-old daughter is an expression of his sincere love for her, and, therefore, who better than he could teach her about sexual love. In general, certain internal precipitants such as stress, anxiety, self-esteem problems, and mood-altering substance-abuse may intensify deviant sexual fantasies or predilections. External circumstances such as exist in dysfunctional families with unavailable mothers, or in occupational contexts with available victims, when interacting with the individual's internal factors, can result in the individual's heightened vulnerability to engage in the deviant sexual pattern. This pattern consists of a chain of internal and external events which comprise a linkage of "triggering" risk factors that culminate in the sexual acting out. In cases of insufficient self-control with ongoing urges to act out, particularly in those paraphiliacs who have victimized others, eg, pedophiles, the clinician must ascertain the patient's current contact with a potential victim and the patient's response to the admonition to immediately avoid or ameliorate the identified risk factors.[11]

PSYCHODYNAMIC FORMULATION

The psychodynamic assessment is basically an in-depth inquiry into the nature of how the sexual symptomatology is related to and embedded within core characterological and interpersonal dynamics. This investigation should include eliciting the quality of early object relations, the development of gender identity and role, the negotiation of the oedipal stage, the genesis of a sense of self and personal identity, the description of the emotional tone of familial interrelationships with emphasis on the presence of seductions, victimization, or abuse, and finally, the depiction of formative extrafamilial, peer relationships. During the course of this inquiry the patient's capacity for insight and psychological-mindedness, which have implications for the nature of further assessment and treatment, become evident.[12]

Obviously, the elicitation of psychodynamic factors overlaps with the detailed sex history. Inasmuch as such key factors as sexual fantasy material, masturbatory activity, and initiation of sexual behavior are inherently enmeshed within the framework of characterological and interpersonal development, the psychodynamic focus can serve to enhance our understanding of the sexual history. In effect, the meaning of the deviant sexual behavior can be psychodynamically understood as symptomatic or derivative of psychological processes, often of an unconscious nature. This psychodynamic data permit the clinician to consider a preliminary formulation of the case.

SPECIALIZED PSYCHOLOGICAL TESTING

There are a variety of specialized psychological testing instruments that can be used to assess various aspects of the paraphiliac's sexual functioning. These specialized techniques are essentially self-reports, and as is the case in all self-reports, depend upon the truthfulness of the examinee. Basically, there are two kinds of self-reports: the first kind contains unidimensional scales that are short and restricted in obtaining information; the second kind consists of multidimensional inventories and questionnaires.[13]

Depending on the nature of the case or the context in which the patient is being assessed, the clinician may want to use some of the following more frequently utilized instruments: (1) Clarke Sexual History Questionnaire[14] for Males (SHQ)—to assess deviant sexual behavior in males; (2) Derogatis Sexual Functioning Inventory (DSFI)[15]—to elicit information in a number of areas of sexual functioning; (3) Sexual Interest Card-Sort—to assess the individual's sexual arousal to specific categories; (4) Pedophile Cognition Scale—to elicit the patient's cognitive distortions; (5) Assault Knowledge Inventory[16,17]—to ascertain the subject's attitudes by using seven different scales, including the rape myth acceptance scale; (6) Adult Self-Expression Scale[18]—to measure the level of the individual's assertiveness. It should be noted that a number of these scales and inventories have been combined in assessment paradigms for use in specialized sex offender assessment and treatment clinics. For example, in the Sex Offender Treatment Clinic at the Psychiatric Institute in New York City, Abel and Becker devised the Sexual Interest Card-Sort and the Pedophile Cognition Scale. They also included most of the above tests in their assessment protocol.

Additionally, a variety of personality inventories and psychosocial testing may be utilized to ascertain characterological patterns of behavior. These may include the Minnesota Multiphasic Personality Inventory (MMPI)-II and the Millon Clinical Multiaxial Inventory (MCMI).

PENILE PLETHYSMOGRAPHIC ASSESSMENT

Although this is a relatively new assessment methodology, erectile measurement studies are being increasingly used.[19] This methodology involves measuring erectile responses to visual and auditory erotic cues in the laboratory setting. Typically, the visual cues are a series of slides depicting paraphilia-related stimuli, varying in sex, age, and in some instances, aggressivity directed against the models shown on the screen. The auditory cues are usually audio-taped narratives of deviant sexual behavior.[20,21] Penile tumescence can be measured volumetrically by a volumetric device,[22] or the widening circumference of the penis can be recorded by several circumferential devices, especially that of the mercury strain gauge.[23] A recent study has indicated that circumference measurement with a mercury strain gauge is a more convenient instrument to use, and may provide as much information as a volumetric device.[24] McConaghy,[25] on the other hand, points out that a volumetric device to measure penile erection (PVR) and circumferential measurement of penile erection (PCR) with a mercury-in-rubber strain gauge transducer do not yield equivalent erection responses. While PVRs measure small penile changes in the early stages of erectile response useful to assess the individual's sexual orientation (heterosexuality vs homosexuality), PCRs record the degree of penile erection to stimuli of 2–10 min durations. Moreover, because of the inconsistent results in studies of erection responses of rapists, McConaghy does not believe that PCRs can validly differentiate rapists from nonrapists.

It should be emphasized that there is some controversy as to the specific uses of erectile measurements. Some specialized sex offender treatment programs routinely use penile plethysmographic assessment, in effect, for all patients,[21] but the majority of sex therapists probably do not utilize this procedure at all. The questions raised about the use of phallometric assessment revolve around the validity of the procedure and its nontraditional means of obtaining useful clinical information. Farkas[26] expresses serious concerns about the internal and external validity of these measures, as well as about the validity of generalizing from these sexual arousal patterns to those outside of the laboratory. In a comprehensive review of the laboratory assessment of sexual preferences, Barbaree[27] concluded that the procedure has "good criterion-related validity (both concurrent and predictive)"[27] (p 117) for the child molester, but not for the rapist. Rosen and Beck[28] point out that deviant sexual arousal does not appear to have the same importance in the diagnosis of paraphiliac disorder. These authors assert that laboratory erectile measurements are somewhat less effective in distinguishing exhibitionists' arousal patterns as compared to pedophiles' arousal patterns. Another limitation of psychophysiologic assessment is the real possibility of response faking. Paraphiliacs appear to be more easily able to suppress responses to deviant stimuli than to voluntarily respond to normative stimuli, which suggests that such assessments involve a greater risk of false negatives. But the possibility of false positive responses also exists: some normal male controls can show arousal to deviant stimuli in the laboratory.[29] "The extent of deviant arousal in some normal subjects should be viewed as an additional caveat against equaling deviant arousal with the proclivity for deviant behavior"[28] (p 217). It should also be mentioned that the reliability of erectile measurements has not yet been adequately tested.

In light of the rather significant limitations of phallometric testing, how can this be of assistance to the clinician? In the courtroom context, Travin et al[30] emphasize that erectile measurement data would constitute a major abuse if it were used as the sole evidence for determining the guilt or innocence of an individual accused of unlawful sexual behavior. On the other hand, some clinicians in the treatment area have found that erectile measurements can be helpful in breaking through the denial patterns common to sex offenders, as well as in monitoring their ongoing treatment responses. In a study of the erectile measurements of 185 subjects who were referred to the Forensic Psychiatry Clinic for assessment of suitability for treatment, Travin et al[30] found that 59 (32%) of these sex offenders initially denied the unlawful behavior. However, when confronted with their positive arousal patterns to deviant stimuli in the laboratory, these sex offenders ultimately acknowledged the paraphiliac disorder. Additionally, erectile measurements can contribute another source of data to corroborate the patient's self-report on his ability to control his deviant sexual inclinations.

Other clinicians, concerned about the psychometric limitations of penile plethysmography, are hesitant to use this methodology. They feel that the data presented under the auspices of an "objective technical instrument," at best will provide information already available from other sources (corroborating agency reports, psychiatric history, and self-reports), and at worst may produce inaccurate, misleading, and unreliable information. In addition, the test may have an intrusive, alienating effect on the patient, which could affect the therapeutic alliance. These issues are particularly germane to clinicians in private practice, when they encounter patients who reveal, during the course of treatment, that they have been engaging in sexually perverse acts.

CONCLUSION

Ultimately, the selection of any or all of the above assessment procedures depends on the clinical context. One needs to keep in mind that there is no universally accepted assessment protocol. Obviously, a specialized treatment clinic would utilize most of the techniques. For the private practitioner involved in the treatment of individual cases, we recommend a more selective approach, and, as needed, consultation with a specialist in the field.

REFERENCES

1. Abel GG, Rouleau JL, Cunningham-Rathner J. Sexually aggressive behavior. In: Curran W, McGarry AL, Shah SA, eds. *Forensic Psychiatry and Psychology: Perspectives and Standards for Interdisciplinary Practice*. Philadelphia, Pa: F.A. Davis; 1986.
2. Berlin FS. Sex offenders: a biomedical perspective and a status report on biomedical treatment. In: Greer JG, Stuart IT, eds. *The Sexual Aggressor: Current Perspective on Treatment*. New York, NY: Van Nostrand Reinhold; 1983.
3. Murphy WD, Coleman EM, Haynes MR. Treatment and evaluation issues with the mentally retarded sex offenders. In: Greer JG, Stuart IR, eds. *The Sexual Aggressor: Current Perspectives on Treatment*. New York, NY: Van Nostrand Reinhold; 1983.
4. Langevin R, Ben-Aron MH, Coulthard R, et al. The effect of alcohol on penile erection. In: Langevin R, ed. *Erotic Preference, Gender Identity, and Aggression in Men: New Research Studies*. Hillsdale, NJ: Lawrence Erlbaum Associates; 1985.
5. Rada R, Kellner R, Laws D, Winslow W. Drinking alcoholism and the mentally disordered sex offender. *Bull Am Acad Psychiatry Law*. 1979;6:296–300.
6. Schmidt CW, Meyer JK, Lucas J. Paraphilias and personality disorders. In: Lion JR, ed. *Personality Disorders: Diagnosis and Management* (revised for DSM-III). 2nd ed. Baltimore, Md: Williams & Wilkins; 1981.
7. Kernberg O. *Borderline Conditions and Pathological Narcissism*. New York, NY: Jason Aronson; 1975.
8. Travin S, Bluestone H, Coleman E, Cullen K, Mellela J. Pedophilia: an update on theory and practice. *Psychiatr Q*. 1985;57:89–103.
9. Travin S. The use of psychiatric expertise in sex offender cases. In: Rosner R, Weinstock R, eds. *Ethical Practice in Psychiatry and the Law*. New York, NY: Plenum Press; 1990.
10. Abel GG, Becker JV, Cunningham-Rathner J. Complications, consent, and cognitions in sex between children and adults. *Int J Law Psychiatry*. 1984;7:89–103.
11. Groth AN. Guidelines for the assessment and management of the offender. In: Burgess AW, Groth AN, Holmstrom LL, Sgroi SM, eds. *Sexual Assault of Children and Adolescents*. Lexington, Mass: Lexington Books; 1978.
12. Protter B, Travin S. Sexual fantasies in the treatment of paraphiliac disorders: a bimodal approach. *Psychiatr Q*. 1987;53:270–297.
13. Conte HR. Development and use of self-report techniques for assessing sexual functioning: a review and critique. *Arch Sex Behav*. 1983;12:555–576.
14. Paitich D, Langevin R, Freeman R, Mann K, Handy L. The Clarke SHQ: a clinical sex history questionnaire for males. *Arch Sex Behav*. 1977;6:421–436.
15. Derogatis LR. Psychological assessment of psychosexual functioning. *The Psychiatric Clinics of North America*. Vol 3. No. 1. Philadelphia, Pa: WB Saunders Company; April 1980.
16. Burt MR. Cultural myths and supports for rape. *J Pers Soc Psychol*. 1980;38:217–230.
17. Burt MR, Alvin RS. Rape myths, rape definitions and probability of conviction. *J Appl Soc Psych*. 1981; 11:212–230.
18. Gay ML, Hollandsworth JG, Golassi JP. An assertiveness inventory for adults. *J Couns Psych*. 1975; 22:340–344.
19. Earls CM, Marshall WL. The current state of technology in the laboratory assess-

ment of sexual arousal patterns. In: Greer JG, Stuart IG, eds. *The Sexual Aggressor: Current Perspectives on Treatment.* New York, NY: Van Nostrand Reinhold; 1983.
20. Abel GG, Becker JV, Blanchard EB, Djendevedjian A. Differentiating sexual aggressives with penile measures. *Crim Justice Behav.* 1978;5:315–332.
21. Abel GG, Becker JV, Murphy WD, Flanagan B. Identifying dangerous child molesters. In: Stuart R, ed. *Violent Behavior—Social Learning Approaches to Prediction, Management and Treatment.* New York, NY: Brunner/Mazel; 1981.
22. Freund, K. A laboratory method for diagnosing predominance of homo- and heteroerotic interest in the male. *Behav Res Ther.* 1963;1:85–93.
23. Bancroft JH, Gwynne Jones HE, Pullan BP. A simple transducer for measuring penile erection with comments on its use in the treatment of sexual disorder. *Behav Res Ther.* 1966;4:239–241.
24. Wheeler D, Rubin HB. A comparison of volumetric and circumferential measures of penile erection. *Arch Sex Behav.* 1987;16:289–299.
25. McConaghy N. Validity and ethics of penile circumference measures of sexual arousal: a critical review. *Arch Sex Behav.* 1989;18:357–369.
26. Farkas GM. Comments on Levin et al and Rosen and Kopel: internal and external validity issues. *J Consult Clin Psychol.* 1978;46:1515–1516.
27. Barbaree HE. Stimulus control of sexual arousal: its role in sexual assault. In: Marshall WL, Laws DR, Barbaree HE, eds. *Handbook of Sexual Assault: Issues, Theories, and Treatment of the Offender.* New York, NY: Plenum Press; 1990.
28. Rosen RC, Beck JG. *Patterns of Sexual Arousal: Psychophysiological Processes and Clinical Applications.* New York, NY: The Guilford Press; 1988.
29. Malamuth NM, Check JVP. Sexual arousal to rape depictions: individual differences. *J Abnormal Psychol.* 1983;92:55–67.
30. Travin S, Cullen K, Melella JT. The use and abuse of erection measurements: a forensic perspective. *Bull Am Acad Psychiatry Law.* 1988;16:235–250.

8

The Treatment of Sexual Perversion

In recent years there have been a variety of approaches to the treatment of sexual perversions. Generally, these approaches can be divided into five main categories: psychodynamic, cognitive-behavioral, relapse prevention, organic, and family systems. The psychodynamic and cognitive-behavioral orientations have largely dominated treatment, inasmuch as both of these approaches purport to treat the full spectrum of paraphiliac disorders. Relapse prevention techniques, which are being used increasingly in specialized treatment programs for sex offenders, can be initiated at the very onset of the treatment encounter.[1] The organic and family systems approaches are somewhat delimited in that each of these perspectives treats a narrower range of deviant sexual disorders. For example, the organic approach, which until recently was confined to the administration of medroxyprogesterone acetate (MPA, Depo-Provera),[2] is used for the seriously acting out and potentially dangerous patient for whom immediate control measures are indicated. The family systems approach has been mostly limited to the advanced stages of the treatment of some incest cases (intrafamilial pedophilia).[3] More recent trends have combined elements of these approaches, including Depo-Provera with cognitive-behavioral approaches,[4] and cognitive-behavioral with psychodynamic approaches.[5] The discussion below will address each of these five categories of treatment in its pure, inclusive form of application. Subsequently, we will attempt to integrate these orientations with a more flexible treatment approach tailored to the individual patient. The authors believe that a bimodal approach that integrates key aspects of the psychodynamic and cognitive-behavioral perspectives represents a core methodology of treatment that is probably most useful to the practicing clinician because of its wider range of applicability. However, the clinician needs to be pragmatic and flexible enough to incorporate organic and family systems approaches when the circumstances of the individual case call for such approaches.

It should be emphasized that group therapy, which is the dominant form of treatment in specialized sex offender treatment programs in America,[6] can offer a variety of nonspecific therapeutic effects such as ventilation, support, positive identification, empathic bonding, and facilitative confrontation. Hence, regardless of one's theoretical orientations, group psychotherapy can be a very useful technique to treat these individuals. Group therapy for paraphiliac patients is consistent with the current pervasive use of group forms of treatment for such repetitive compulsive problems as eating disorders, chemical dependencies, and gambling.

PSYCHODYNAMIC APPROACHES TO PERVERSION

Psychodynamic approaches to treating the sexually perverse patient have evolved with the changing theoretical climates in the field since Freud's[7] (1905) revolutionary early work on the topic. Freud postulated that perversion was the negative of neurosis. But there was general skepticism about the likelihood that the sexually perverse patient could be adequately treated in the psychoanalytic situation. In this early "id psychological" emphasis, the sexual perversion was seen as a raw ego syntonic, pleasure-producing symptom of the drive, undeflected by ego, superego, or defensive structures. As such, the patient had little or no motivation to change. Unlike the suffering neurotic, whose repressed unconscious material waited to be uncovered by the analyst's interpretations, the sexually perverse patient repressed nothing, and acted out his unconscious in such a manner that he had little to gain by giving up his pleasurable symptom. Hence, the therapeutic alliance was undermined, and the analyst's interpretations were rendered impotent.

Subsequently,[5] writers[8,9,10] began to increasingly understand perverse symptoms as serving "defensively-related functions such as general neurotic formation,[8] the shoring up of flaws in the development of a sense of reality,[9] and a regressive adaptation against castration fears"[10] (p 283). Perversion was basically understood as a developmental arrest serving defensive-compromise purposes that centered on oedipal dynamics. More advanced views of perversion, drawing upon elements of ego psychology, still remained within a drive structure model of psychoanalysis. The central meaning of the perversion hinged on regressive defenses against oedipal dynamics (castration anxiety), and the core therapeutic action of psychoanalysis was the exercise of interpretive insight. Case histories of analytic treatment reflecting this sensibility (most of them involving such perversions as fetishisms, exhibitionism, and masochism) repetitively focus on the curative effect of patients gaining insight into oedipal dynamics and origins of their sexual afflictions.

In recent years a relational-structure model of psychoanalysis,[12,13] drawing on elements of later ego psychology, object relations, interpersonal schools, and self psychology, has offered new interpretative strategies to the therapist, and has more directly addressed the patient–analyst relational factors of transference-countertransference as having a significant curative role in psychoanalysis in addition to insight. Sexual perversion, in this more recent perspective, is understood as a means of defending against or repairing earlier disturbed, anxiety-laden relationships, or a fragmented, weakened, or inadequate sense of self or identity. The origins of these problems generally stem from preoedipal sources centering around such core issues as separation-individuation and the development of a cohesive sense of self. The perversion is thus understood as a shoring-up maneuver that utilizes conscious sexualization as a mood-altering self-esteem regulatory device to stave off unsettling and dysphoric affects that derive from childhood interpersonal abandonments, intrusions, and misattunements. Early child sexual traumata and the child's subtle enactment of their parents' unconscious erotic conflicts and scripts may be amongst the early disturbed relationship patterns that are prominent in the etiology of the perversion.

Contemporary psychodynamic approaches to the perverse patient are essentially consistent with the psychodynamic approaches to treatment of other compulsive disorders that are believed to be derivative of characterological pathology. Among them are eating, gambling, and substance abuse disorders. In the contemporary relational schools, however, character is seen as a complicated layering of defensive structures that mediate struggles around the formation of self and identity in the context of relational patterns with the other, rather than as the unidimensional substrate of instinctual energies. The achievement of states such as those of attachment and security has a primary dynamic of its own, a dynamic not reducible to drive gratification. Consequently, the treatment of the sexually perverse patient is a treatment of characterological issues (understood in this large relational framework), and one's focus is always attuned to what meaning the perverse act has and how it is embedded in the total characterological picture of the individual. Psychodynamic character diagnosis and assessment are therefore inherently intertwined with treatment. The patient's characterological development is key to how the act of perversion is appropriated in his life adjustment patterns.[14] The neurotic, for example, may utilize the perverse act to enhance genital potency while defending against fears of castration; the narcissistically oriented character may act on his perversion as a soothing repair of self defects and relational trauma; and the borderline may manifest polymorphous perverse behavior in the context of ego fragmentation and impulsive deficits. Drawing upon widely accepted studies in character structures such as those of Kernberg[15,16] and Kohut,[17,18] psychoanalytic theorists have suggested the ways in which sexual perversion is embedded within the characterological development of sexually perverse patients. The dynamic psychotherapist is also acutely interested in the inner sexual fantasy life of these individuals. The psychotherapist needs to inquire particularly into the unconscious significance of sexual fantasy material and how this relates to the etiology of character pathology.

Within the relational-structure perspective, the therapeutic action of psychodynamic therapy lies not only in uncovering the meaning of the sexual perversion, but also in utilizing the leverage of the therapist's relationship to the patient in affecting characterological changes. This, in turn, impacts on the perverse symptomatology. A restorative-nurturant approach, drawing on self psychological and object relations schools, advocates that the therapist, in effect, offers a kind of corrective emotional experience to the patient, by consolidating an empathic bond that compensates for or restores missing internal structures of the self that are in developmental arrest. The therapist needs to let specific archaic transference states variously called "narcissistic transferences" or "self object transference," wherein a maturational growth process can be initiated in the therapy, flourish by his facilitative, empathic stance. Perverse sexual acting out or distressing urges, as they may occur during the course of treatment, can be understood as a search for compensatory self objects buttressing up a shaky sense of self. The therapist needs to understand how these impulses may be related to empathic breaks or misattunements in the transference. The therapist then needs to interpret this process while investigating the nature of the affective state that triggered the perverse behavior or impulses. Efforts to reconstruct earlier analogs to such subjective states need to be undertaken with the goal of the patient's acquiring greater internal capacity to contain and delay these unsettling affective states rather than act on them in a compulsive fashion. The psychoanalyst's steady and reliable presence as a model for containment is vital to this process. In addition, the therapist's humanizing and pacifying role helps the patient to develop a more intimate, whole object relationship to the therapist over time. This facilitates the enrichment of the patient's internal structural world. As a result, the patient is better able to develop more mature sexual relationships in his life.

A more interpersonal-interactive technique, while overlapping with the above approach, more keenly focuses on the interactive nature of transference-countertransference patterns in the analytic process.[19] In this technique, the therapist eschews seeing characterological problems solely as arrests in development in which the analyst plays a nurturing, caretaking role making up for undeveloped features of personality. This "developmental tilt view" minimizes the here and now defensive features of both characterological patterns and perverse symptomatology.[20] The interpersonal-interactive approach emphasizes the analyst's flexibility in monitoring the manner in which the analyst is being related to by the patient in the therapy session. This monitoring is accomplished by accessing the transference-countertransference patterns. It provides vital information in regard to the analogs of the patient's early interpersonal relationships as well as the patient's present interpersonal relationships. The main features of the therapeutic action in the treatment are the psychotherapist's interpretations centered on crucial features of the transference-countertransference matrix, and the psychotherapist's capacity to resist being transformed into relating in a manner indicative of older pathogenic relationships. If the psychotherapist makes transferential interpretations that truly reflect what is going on in the present relationship between the psychotherapist and the patient, this provides the most emotionally effective resonance to the patient's core characterologic-relational way of being.

Dynamic group therapy, probably amongst the most widely used orientations in group treatment, is based upon the utilization of insight and the enactment of transferential patterns in the group process. Many of the above-mentioned features of group therapy (support, ventilation, helpful confrontation) have their roots in psychodynamically based concepts of insight, self-disclosure, and the leverage of the therapeutic alliance.[21] Of particular importance is the use of the group community as a self object which provides mirroring and empathic features to the besieged self.[18] This group process may be needed by some of the more severe paraphiliac patients who, because of their alienation from society, receive the support of group members with the message that others suffer from similar disorders. Another important feature of the group process is the role of confrontation in facilitating the individual's acknowledgment of a sense of responsibility for the paraphiliac activity. This can be accomplished by breaking through the patient's defense patterns, which often include denial, rationalization, and externalization. It is ultimately vital that the individual own up to his existential guilt entailed in his perverse activities, which have been both self-destructive and harmful to others. Open disclosure in the group format can also be instrumental in working through the issue of shame that is so central to the characterology of many of these patients.

It should be pointed out that an area of controversy in dynamic psychotherapy, particularly in individual psychotherapy, is the issue of how directly the perverse symptomatology needs to be confronted in the treatment, and how actively the psychotherapist needs to press the patient to give up the symptom. Many psychoanalysts would generally take a neutral-empathic stance toward the perverse patient, with the understanding that the patient can only let go of the symptom when he is characterologically ready to do so. To more actively intervene with techniques to address change of the sexual symptomatology per se, would undermine the essential nondirective, exploratory nature of the psychoanalysis, as well as hinder the development of a therapeutic alliance. More recent therapies that have utilized dynamic orientations have taken a more active, directive approach to perverse symptomatology with the goal of effecting more immediate behavioral changes.[5] These approaches have drawn on the methodologies of short-term focused dynamic psychotherapy and have been integrated with other therapeutic orientations in a multimodal manner. (This will be discussed in more detail in the next chapter.) When issues of self-control are paramount in the paraphiliac disorder, as clearly would be the case in certain types of sex offenders, a more active and directive approach is pragmatically necessary.

COGNITIVE-BEHAVIORAL APPROACHES TO PERVERSION

Cognitive-behavioral approaches to the treatment of paraphiliac disorders utilize a broad range of therapeutic interventions that are loosely derived from conditioning and social learning perspectives, as well as from theories of cognition. Cognitive-behavioral interventions have been used in virtually the full spectrum of psychological disorders and behavioral problems. These interventions embrace a diverse set of techniques that are practical, task-oriented, and educative in nature. Essentially, the cognitive-behavioral treatment paradigm is based upon a psychosocial-deficit model of functioning. That is, the individual's problems are understood as a series of deficits or incompetencies in various areas of behavior. These deficiencies are viewed as derived from maladaptive social learning patterns that therefore can be ameliorated by a variety of psychoeducative interventions. Because of the emphasis on observable or measurable responses to the interventions, cognitive-behavioral techniques lend themselves to empirical outcome studies.

Historically, behavioral therapists had experimented with single-task interventions directly derived from classical or operant conditioning principles that generally targeted the subject's sexual preference, eg, aversion therapy utilizing electroshocks to alter the paraphiliac's arousal pattern. During the past twenty years more inclusive cognitive-behavioral paradigms that incorporate a variety of cognitively mediated intervention techniques have been responsible for the evolution of a number of integrated, comprehensive treatment programs. This expansion of cognitive-behavioral intervention techniques addresses the multifactorial nature of deviant sexual disorders. Treatment for paraphiliac disorders can be grouped into four major categories defined by their specific purposes and goals: self-control techniques, stress-management techniques, cognitive restructuring techniques, and social rehabilitative techniques.

Self-Control Techniques

Self-control techniques include a variety of self-administered methods or procedures that the individual can utilize in order to gain control over his deviant fantasies, urges, and activities. These techniques can be characterized as varying on a continuum from the least to the most intrusive. Knopp[22] enumerates some commonly used less intrusive operations such as thought-shifting, which entails the subject's diverting his deviant sexual thoughts to nonsexual topics, possibly with the aide of an external cue such as snapping a wrist rubberband; thought-stopping, which means that the subject is able to stop the chain of sexual associative thoughts with the aide of a self-commanding cue, for example, using the word "stop" or "switch"; and impulse charting, which consists of the subject's monitoring closely in a logbook his deviant thoughts and urges. Additional self-control measures that are somewhat more intrusive include covert sensitization and masturbatory satiation. *Covert sensitization* was introduced by Gold and Neufeld[23] in 1965 for the treatment of a homosexual man. The technique was named "covert sensitization" by Cautela,[24] who also used it to treat homosexuality. Basically, covert sensitization involves the subject's pairing in his mind the chain of behavior leading up to, but not including, the deviant sexual act, with the aversive consequences generated by his own personal experiences. Initially, the patient needs to delineate the internal and external triggering events that are linked in a sequential chain that culminates in the deviant sexual act. One important purpose of this delineation is to make the patient aware that, in the process of the sexual offense, there is a whole series of escalating, intervening steps in which the patient is both an actor and reactor. The patient becomes aware that he is not merely a passive participant who is overtaken by mystifying impulses. The pairing of this sequential chain with aversive consequences serves to condition the patient to painful associations instead of pleasurable ones so as to extinguish the deviant sexual behavior. It is common to have the patient make audio tapes of the procedure as homework assignments. Usually the sequence consists of a short description of a neutral scene, followed by a narrative of a chain of linking behaviors, which is then followed by an aversive scene. During this treatment phase, some therapists add a short award scene after the aversive scene. In the award scene, the patient verbalizes the important benefits he hopes will occur if he continues treatment, so that he may be encouraged to do so. The patient is asked to bring the tape back to the therapy sessions for critical review, and also as verification that he did the assigned cognitive-behavioral task. In general, the patient is expected to complete a minimum of five tapes consisting of five sequential narratives on each side, but it is emphasized that, depending on the circumstances, there is no maximum number in order for the individual to achieve self-control.

Masturbatory satiation is a procedure introduced by Marshall.[25] It was developed for the purpose of linking boredom and satiation effects with the paraphiliac's deviant fantasies. Basically, the patient is asked to masturbate for 10 minutes or until ejaculation while fantasizing about a mutually consenting sexual activity, and then to continue to masturbate for the next 50 minutes using a hierarchy from the most to the least of 4 or 5 deviant sexual preferences as fantasy material. The one hour of continuous masturbation is thus divided into a 10-minute segment of a normative scene and 4 or 5 segments of deviant sexual scenes. The individual is expected to verbalize the scenes into a tape recorder, and to bring the audiotape back to the therapy sessions in order to have the procedure monitored and critiqued. In a number of case studies, this technique has been shown to substantially reduce deviant sexual arousal patterns.

Stress Management

The next cognitive-behavioral intervention technique that we will discuss is that of stress management. Inasmuch as stress is contributory to much symptomatic sexual acting out behavior, an important intervention with many of these patients is the utilization of stress-management techniques. Specifically, stressful events or experiences can be triggers in the chain of behaviors leading up to the paraphiliac act. Consequently, if the individual develops techniques to better cope with stress, this may be helpful in reducing his deviant sexual behavior. Stress management techniques can be viewed as comprising several basic approaches including (1) those of a more cognitive nature, such as correcting distortions or irrational ideas; (2) those of a more physical-behavioral nature, such as breathing techniques, progressive relaxation, and autogenic techniques; (teaching one's body to respond to verbal commands of relaxation) and (3) a combination of two approaches, for example, utilizing stress-inoculation training (where the individual constructs a hierarchy of stressful events) and matching these events with new ways of coping. The interested reader can be referred to

Davis, Eshelman, and McKay's book, *The Relaxation & Stress Reduction Workbook*[26] for a practical introduction and review of these techniques.

Cognitive Restructuring

Cognitive restructuring, or the modification of cognitive distortions, is widely used to correct faulty thinking patterns or attitudes that contribute to, as well as sustain, the ongoing paraphiliac behavior. Cognitive distortions enable the paraphiliac individual to utilize a wide variety of defensive mechanisms, including denial, rationalization, minimalization, and projection, all of which serve to justify the behavior in the mind of the offender. In extreme instances, some of these cognitive distortions have a delusional-like quality to them. As an example, an incest pedophile may claim that he had sexual intercourse with his 8-year-old daughter because she was acting seductively toward him. In contrast to this idiosyncratic distortion of events, many sex offenders partake in culturally shared and male-oriented myths in the culture at large, such as those concerning rape against or dehumanizing views toward women. Cognitive restructuring techniques are largely psychoeducational in nature. The therapist confronts the patient in a benign, socratic manner with the goal of having the patient identify for himself his distortions and how he utilizes them in the maintenance of his deviant sexual behavior. The therapist provides corrective feedback and appropriate information. An important technique in cognitive restructuring is empathy training, that can be used to help the patient understand how his behavior impacts profoundly on the victim. Sometimes victims' counselors are invited into the group to report on the kinds of experiences that victims undergo in their ordeal. In addition, the therapist may recommend books, films, and so forth, in order to sensitize the offender to victimization experiences.

Social Rehabilitative Techniques

Numerous authors[27,28] have observed that paraphiliac individuals have a variety of social and interpersonal deficits. Consequently, specialized treatment programs have incorporated an assortment of social rehabilitative techniques to address those deficiencies in their clients. The individual practitioner may integrate some of these techniques chosen to fit the particularities and pragmatic considerations of the individual case. McKay, Davis, and Fanning[29] have discussed in a practical guidebook a variety of communication skills that they have incorporated into a comprehensive psychoeducational program to improve interpersonal effectiveness. These skills include the capacity to listen, improve self-disclosure, use body language and paralanguage (pitch, resonances, articulation, tempo, volume, and rhythm), develop sensitivity to hidden agendas in communicating with others, make contact with strangers, and disavow the abuse of prejudgment. Of particular interest for treating paraphiliacs would be guidelines for the improvement of sexual communication with the individual's partner, or for those individuals not in a relationship, to be able to initiate and sustain a peer-appropriate sexual relationship. Social-skills training modules frequently utilize such well-known techniques as modeling, role-playing, homework assignments for the person to rehearse and try out new skills in the real world, and book assignments and video demonstrations to impart helpful information.

A major component of socials-skills training is the acquisition of assertiveness skills. In contrast to aggressiveness, assertiveness means that the individual has a perfect right to express his feelings and wishes as long as he does not tread on the rights of others. Typically, the individual's reactions to a range of situations and experiences are explored in order to determine specific areas of ineffectual behaviors. Ineffectual behaviors often reflect certain myths, mistaken assumptions, or cognitive distortions that undermine the individual's capacity to assert his legitimate right to express his feelings honestly and directly. Assertiveness training can often be a source of stress reduction in interpersonal transactions.

Sex Education

Many paraphiliacs are misinformed about some of the basic facts of human sexuality. Moreover, a significant number of these individuals suffer from a variety of sexual dysfunctional disorders. That is, those paraphiliacs who show some erotic preference to peer-appropriate partners often experience such problems as premature erection and ejaculation difficulties. Misinformation and sexual dysfunction contribute to the paraphiliac's stress and level of frustration and lower his self-esteem regarding his sense of manhood. By demystifying and correcting distortions about sexual functioning, sex education attempts to reverse this trend in the paraphiliac individual. Sexual dysfunctions may be treated by the primary therapist, or the patient may be referred to a specialist in this area.

RELAPSE PREVENTION WITH SEXUAL PERVERSION

In recent years, relapse prevention has achieved increasing prominence in the treatment of a variety of compulsive disorders including gambling, substance abuse, smoking, and eating disorders. Because paraphiliac disorders are considered to be forms of compulsive sexual behavior consisting of recurrent fantasies, urges, and activities, relapse prevention has been applied to these clinical entities.[1] However, despite initial success in treating these compulsive disorders, therapists are concerned about the long-term maintenance of remission. Clearly compulsively harmful perverse behavior (for example, pedophilic acting-out behavior) requires more relapse prevention monitoring than do cases of less harmful and less compulsive behavior (for example, episodic fantasies about cross-dressing). It seems probable that many clinicians who have treated compulsive disorders intuitively utilized a number of relapse-prevention techniques, but these clinicians did not label these techniques as such. Indeed, many of the principles of relapse prevention inhere within the variety of existing cognitive-behavioral treatment regimens.

According to George and Marlatt,[30] "relapse prevention is a self-control program designed to teach individuals who are trying to change their behavior how to anticipate and cope with the problem of relapse.... Based on social cognitive principles, relapse prevention has a psychoeducational thrust that combines behavioral skill-training procedures with cognitive intervention techniques" (p 2). George and Marlatt differentiate between the terms "lapse" and "relapse" when speaking of sex offenders. "The term lapse will refer to any occurrence of willful and elaborate fantasizing about sexual offending or any return to sources of stimulation ... the term relapse will refer to any occurrence of a sexual offense ... " (p 6). Among the reported predispositions to relapse in the various addictions are such "high-risk situations (HRS)" (p 7) as negative emotional states, interpersonal conflicts, and social pressures. If the individual has not developed effective coping mechanisms, then these high-risk situations will likely lead to either a lapse or a relapse. Without the ability to adequately cope, the individual develops an increased sense of deprivation and begins to experience a need for immediate gratification. The individual could then lapse by engaging in deviant sexual fantasies or the antecedent behaviors in the chain that leads up to the deviant act itself. The individual may rationalize and deny his real intention in these escalating sequences of activities by considering them to be only "apparently irrelevant decision (AIDS)" (p 27). How the individual interprets and reacts to this lapse is termed "abstinence (or rule) violation effect (AVE)" (p 9). George and Marlatt[30] emphasize that a "cognitive restructuring antidote" for this abstinence violation effect should contain the following four principles:

1. "The occurrence of a single slip does not indicate treatment failure and inevitable relapse.
2. The slip should be reviewed as a reasonable mistake in learning how to maintain a self-control program.
3. Overemphasis on the postslip feelings of guilt and conflict ... can precipitate further indulgence.
4. Blaming the slip on personal weakness ... can create a self-fulfilling prophecy that promotes further indulgence" (p 24).

The suggested-relapse prevention techniques include identifying risk factors, self-monitoring these factors closely, developing coping strategies for high-risk situations, and relapse rehearsal of successful coping procedures. There may be emphasis on promoting a positive lifestyle and on enhancing empathy for sex-abuse victims. Depending on the patient and the treatment context, the variety of these techniques can be flexibly integrated. In a sex offender treatment program, we recommend that relapse prevention commence at the very start of treatment. Indeed, some programs incorporate frequent contacts with probation, parole, and family as part of their protocol for relapse prevention. In private practice, the therapist can choose selectively among these techniques on a case-by-case basis.

ORGANIC APPROACHES TO SEXUAL PERVERSION

Bradford[31] has divided organic treatment for male sex offenders into three main groups: antiandrogen or other hormonal agents, surgical castration, and stereotaxic neurosurgery. More recently there have been reports in the literature about the treatment of paraphiliac and nonparaphiliac sexual addiction with antidepressant drugs such as fluoxatine (Prozac).[32]

Because surgical castration and stereotaxic neurosurgery for the treatment of sex offenders in this country are only of academic interest, we will only mention them briefly. Surgical castration has been reported by Heim in 1979 as both variable and unreliable. He found that 40% of 20 castrated men continued to have sexual intercourse 3 to 7 years after the surgery.[33] Bradford,[31] on the other hand, comments that castration unquestionably "has a massive impact on sexual recidivism in the post-castration stage" (p 368). In regard to stereotaxic neurosurgery, Rieber and Sigusch[34] reviewed the reports on cases of stereotaxic hypothalamotomies performed on 74 men and one woman from 1962 to 1979 in the Federal Republic of Germany. They concluded that there were too many methodological errors and inadequacies for the findings to be used. Schmidt and Schorsch[35] also concluded that stereotaxic hypothalamotomic surgery was a highly questionable procedure. Bradford[31] asserts that "at this stage it is unlikely that psychosurgical techniques are going to play any major role in the treatment of sexual deviation..." (p 370).

Since the use of cyproterone acetate (CPA) is not permitted in this country, we will focus on the other major androgen-depleting agent, medroxyprogesterone acetate (MPA, Depo-Provera). Money, Migeon, and Rivarola were the first researchers to experiment with MPA in the treatment of sexual deviancy.[36] MPA has become the most frequently used drug for the experimental treatment of paraphiliac disorders in the United States.[37] It is administered in a dosage of 300–400 mg intramuscularly every 7 to 10 days in order to reduce the plasma testosterone level. Some of the common side effects of the drug include hypertension, weight gain, and mild lethargy. There is a possibility of more serious adverse effects such as hyperglycemia, thrombophlebitis, and pulmonary embolism. In addition, there are reports of its producing breast cancer in female beagle dogs. A major criticism of MPA is that, while it reduces the intensity of the sexual drive, it does not alter the direction of the drive. If the medication is discontinued, after 7–10 days, the patient's libido and his erectile and ejaculatory capacities begin to return, as does the original deviant sexual drive.

FAMILY SYSTEMS APPROACH TO SEXUAL PERVERSION

The underlying assumption of a family systems approach is that there are dynamic-systemic interactions among family members that contribute to the development of the identified patient's symptomatic problem, and that serve as well to maintain the familial unit in a homeostatic balance. Family therapy—the practical modality of the systems approach to treatment—has been utilized in virtually all psychiatric disorders. In the area of paraphiliac symptomatology, a family systems perspective can be illuminating; it can enable an understanding of how the family system may be contributory to the disorder. Clinical experience has indicated that many sexually disordered individuals have come from dysfunctional families in which there has been physical, sexual, or emotional abuse. Although a systems perspective can increase our understanding of etiology, the actual application of treatment, utilizing a family systems approach, has been quite delimited. For the most part, a family systems approach has been confined to incest cases.[38]

Clinicians who have treated cases of father–daughter incest have described some of the following characteristics in the dysfunctional family: a mother–daughter role reversal with the daughter becoming a wife figure in the household; a weak, ineffectual mother who has unconscious feelings of hostility and dependence toward the daughter; a pseudomature daughter who seeks nurturance from the father as a result of rejection from the mother; sexual incompatibility between the parents; overwhelming fears of separation, disintegration, and abandonment shared by all family members; and lack of support, protection, and in some extreme instances, collusion in the family with the daughter assuming a sexual role with the father. It also should be mentioned that many of these dysfunctional families are isolated from the community at large.

Most important, we must emphasize that though family dynamics may be operative and contributory in some instances to the sexual acting out, these dynamic factors do not in any way excuse the behavior of the offender. Essentially the family dysfunctional system can be understood as creating an enabling set of conditions, which intereact with the offender's intrapsychic processes. But as is the case with any other piece of symptomatic behavior, the individual needs to exercise control of, and responsibility for, his actions.

The issues of whether and when to bring the traumatized incest family together for therapeutic intervention is an extremely controversial subject. As Herman[39] has noted, immediately upon disclosure, the incestuous family is too traumatized and fragmented for any considerations of family therapy. It is only after the mother gains strength and self-esteem and improves her coping mechanism, the child becomes less distressed and guilty and is able to continue normal development, and the father is well along in his own specialized treatment, that the reunification of the family and its engagement in family therapy can be considered. It needs to be emphasized that many families dissolve and never enter family therapy, and those that do enter family therapy may eventually go the route of separation. In some instances, family therapy may help to achieve a more worked through separation that is to the psychological advantage of all members of the family unit.

In a broader sense of a systems approach, such modalities of therapeutic intervention as couples' therapy, or obtaining the cooperation of family members (eg, the mother of a juvenile sexual offender), can be helpful adjunctive techniques. Interactional conflicts between husband and wife may generate sufficient tension and stress to serve as precipitants for the acting-out sexual behavior. The mechanism of so-called codependence, that is, the spouses's unconscious investment in the maintenance of the sexual addictive acting out, is an area of inquiry worth investigating. In some instances, another advantage of adjunctive couples' therapy is to provide educational counseling to the wife about the nature of the deviant sexual disorder in order to allay her anxiety and to obtain her support and cooperation in the treatment process. Such problems as sexual miscommunication and dysfunction can be addressed in the couples' sessions.

CONCLUSION

In this chapter we have summarized what we consider to be the five basic approaches to the treatment of deviant sexuality. It is important to reemphasize that there is as yet no definitive treatment model that applies across all paraphiliac disorders. Although this may be true to some extent with other clinical entities, the treatment of deviant sexuality takes on particular significance because the disorder often entails victimization of other persons. Hence, there may be pressures from various quarters to ensure a more certain treatment outcome, that is, the cessation of the sexual acting out. This is why relapse prevention is such an important factor in treatment. Although relapse-prevention techniques have been more explicitly addressed within the cognitive-behavioral paradigm, the basic principle of anticipating and preventing future sexual acting out has application in all the approaches described above.

It is the point of view of the present authors that, indeed, there is an area of expertise and specialization in treating the paraphiliac individual. This expertise takes the form of acquiring familiarity and experience with the basic treatment approaches discussed above in order to be able to draw upon the (possibly several) approaches best suited to each individual case. In our clinical experience, we have found that the most pragmatic and suitable approach for the widest range of patients has been an integration of the cognitive-behavioral and psychodynamic treatment approaches combined with relapse-prevention techniques integrated with both these core modalities.

REFERENCES

1. Laws DR, ed. *Relapse Prevention with Sex Offenders*. New York, NY: The Guilford Press; 1989.
2. Berlin FS, Meinecke CF. Treatment of sex offenders with antiandrogenic medication: conceptualization, review of treatment modalities, and preliminary findings. *Am J Psychiatry*. 1981;138:601 607.
3. Herman J. Recognition and treatment of incestuous families. In: Barnard CP, ed. *Families, Incest, and Therapy. International Journal of Family Therapy*. 1983; Vol 5. No 2. 81–91.
4. Marshall WL, Eccles A. Issues in clinical practice with sex offenders. *J Interpersonal Violence*. 1991;6:68–93.
5. Protter B, Travin S. Sexual fantasies in the treatment of paraphiliac disorders: a bimodal approach. *Psychiatr Q*. 1985;58:270–297.
6. Burzecki M, Wormith JS. A survey of treatment programs for sex offenders in North America. *Canad Psych*. 1987;28:30–44.
7. Freud S. Three essays on the theory of sexuality. In: Strachey J, ed. Standard Edition. Vol 7. London, England: Hogarth Press; 1905; 125–243.
8. Sachs H, Goldberg RB, trans. On the genesis of perversions. *Psychoanal Q*. 1986;LV:477–488.
9. Glover E. The relation of perversion formation to the development of reality sense. *Int J Psycho anal*. 1933;14:486–504.
10. Bak R. Aggression and perversion. In: Lorand S, Balint M, eds. *Perversions: Psychodynamics and Therapy*. New York, NY: Random House; 1956.
11. Gillespie WH. The general theory of sexual perversion. *Int J Psychoanal*. 1956;37:396–403.
12. Greenberg J, Mitchell S. *Object Relations in Psychoanalysis*. Cambridge, Mass: Harvard University Press; 1987.
13. Mitchell SA. *Relational Concepts in Psychoanalysis: An Integration*. Cambridge, Mass: Harvard University Press; 1988.
14. Gabbard GO. *Psychodynamic Psychiatry in Clinical Practice*. Washington, DC: American Psychiatric Press Inc; 1990.
15. Kernberg O. *Borderline Conditions and Pathological Narcissism*. New York, NY: Jason Aronson Inc; 1975.

16. Kernberg O. *Severe Personality Disorders: Psychotherapeutic Strategies*. New Haven, Conn: Yale University Press; 1984.
17. Kohut H. *The Analysis of the Self*. New York, NY: International Universities Press; 1971.
18. Kohut H. *The Restoration of the Self*. New York, NY: International Universities Press; 1977.
19. Levenson E. *The Ambiguity of Change*. New York, NY: Basic Books; 1983.
20. Mitchell SA. Object relations theories and the developmental tilt. *Contemp Psychoanal*. 1984;20:473–499.
21. Yalom ID. *The Theory and Practice of Group Psychotherapy*. 2nd ed. New York, NY: Basic Books Inc; 1975.
22. Knopp FH. *Retraining Adult Sex Offenders: Methods and Models*. Syracuse, NY: Safer Society Press; 1984.
23. Gold SA, Neufeld IL. A learning approach to the treatment of homosexuality. *Behav Res Ther*. 1965;3:201–204.
24. Cautela JR. Covert sensitization. *Psychol Rec*. 1967;20:459–468.
25. Marshall WL. Satiation therapy: a procedure for reducing deviant sexual arousal. *J App Behav Anal*. 1979;12:10–22.
26. Davis M, Eshelman ER, McKay M. *The Relaxation & Stress Reduction Workbook*. 3rd ed. Oakland, Calif: New Harbinger Publications Inc; 1988.
27. Marshall WL, McKnight RD. An integrated treatment program for sexual offenders. *Canad Psychiatr Assoc J*. 1975;20:133–138.
28. Whitman WP, Quinsey VL. Heterosocial skills training for institutionalized rapists and child molesters. *Canad J Behav Sci*. 1981;13:105–114.
29. McKay M, Davis M, Fanning P. *Messages: The Communication Skills Book*. Oakland, Calif: New Harbinger Publications Inc; 1983.
30. George WH, Marlatt GA. Introduction. In: Laws RD, ed. *Relapse Prevention with Sex Offenders*. New York, NY: The Guilford Press; 1989:1–31.
31. Bradford JMW. Organic treatments for the male sexual offender. *Behav Sci Law*. 1985;3:355–375.
32. Kafka MP. Successful antidepressant treatment of nonparaphilic sexual addictions and paraphilias in men. *J Clin Psychiatry*. 1991;52:60–65.
33. Heim N, Jursch CJ. Castration for sex offenders: treatment or punishment? A review and critique of recent European literature. *Arch Sex Behav*. 1979;8:281–304.
34. Rieber I, Sigusch V. Psychosurgery on sex offenders and sexual deviants in West Germany. *Arch Sex Behav*. 1979;8:523–527.
35. Schmidt G, Schorsch E. Psychosurgery of sexually deviant patients: review and analysis of new empirical findings. *Arch Sex Behav*. 1981;10:301–323.
36. Money J. The therapeutic use of androgen-depleting hormone. In: Resnick HLP, Wolfgang ME, eds. *Treatment of the Sex Offender. International Psychiatry Clinics*. Vol 8. No 4. Boston, Md: Little Brown & Co; 1972; 165–174.
37. Berlin FS, Meinecke CF. Treatment of sex offenders with antiandrogenic medication: conceptualization review of treatment modalities, and preliminary findings. *Am J Psychiatry*. 1981;138:601–607.
38. Reposa RF, Zuelzer MB. Family therapy with incest. In: Barnard CP, ed. *Families, Incest, and Therapy*. A Special Issue of International Journal of Family Therapy. Vol 5. No 2; Summer, 1983.
39. Herman J. Recognition and treatment of incestuous families. In: Barnard CP, ed. *Families, Incest, and Therapy*. A Special Issue of International Journal of Family Therapy. Vol 5. No 2; Summer, 1983.

9

Integrative Perspectives on Treating Sexual Perversion

For a number of years, the present authors have utilized an integrative approach, which is essentially bimodal in nature, in the treatment of sexual perversions.[1] This bimodal approach is based on the proposition that key components of both the cognitive-behavioral and psychodynamic paradigms can be effectively integrated. A central feature of this approach is the focus on fantasy material, both for understanding the nature of the sexual perversion and as the crucial axis of therapeutic intervention in the application of treatment.

Before turning to the integrative approach that we have developed, it is useful to review briefly the general role of fantasy in both the psychodynamic and cognitive-behavioral treatment paradigms, and particularly as applied to the treatment of the sexually perverse disorders. As outlined in Chapter 6 (this volume), unconscious material related to perverse sexual fantasy does not necessarily have a drive-structure base. Indeed, contemporary psychodynamic trends have postulated a host of unconscious-relational structure meanings concerning such issues as the need for human attachment, the formation of selfhood and identity, the need for security, the sense of safety, and so forth. The meanings attributed to these issues by the individual can be encapsulated in enduring idiosyncratic fantasy themata that are operative in all the topographical levels—conscious, preconscious, and unconscious. For the paraphiliac individual, the conscious, perverse fantasies have unique representational values that psychically resonate to preconscious and unconscious meaning.

Initially, behavioral therapists treating paraphiliac individuals did not fully appreciate the importance of fantasy material in treatment.[2] With behavioral therapists' increasing appreciation of cognitive processes in treatment,[3] the sexual specialists among them developed a growing awareness of the significance of cognitive processes in the form of conscious fantasies. However, in contrast to psychodynamic therapists, cognitive-behavioral therapists restrict themselves to conscious fantasy material and observable behavior.

The directive focus on fantasy material in the treatment of sexual perversions to effect changes has, in recent years, come under increased discussion. Abel and Blanchard,[2] writing from a cognitive-behavioral treatment orientation, describe the several conceptualizations of fantasy as (a) a dependent variable (ie, the fantasy changes only after treatment affects the basic causal phenomenon); (b) an intervening variable (ie, a change in one variable causes a change in the deviant fantasy, which then affects the behavior); and (c) an independent variable (ie, a direct alteration of the fantasy can change the behavior). Abel and Blanchard state that the conceptualization of fantasy as an independent variable is being used by the more recent behavioral technologies. Thus, the alteration of the independent variable of "conscious fantasy" through various cognitive-behavioral techniques effects a change in the overt sexual behavior. Despite this emphasis on conscious fantasy material, some authors have acknowledged the significance of unconscious fantasy processes as being therapeutically operative in cognitive-behavioral therapy. In this regard, Mendelsohn and Silverman[4] have written about the connection between the therapeutic efficacy of behavioral therapy and unconscious fantasy, and suggested that the success of behavioral therapy may be attributed to the activation of unconscious fantasy material. Messer[5] has provided an example in the case of assertiveness training, when the behavioral therapist may be mobilizing the patient's assertiveness toward his father by permitting the patient to express partially an unconscious fantasy of harming his father and thereby "preparing the client for the expression and gratification of milder forms of the wish" (p 1266).

Although the psychodynamic approach has long been considered a nondirective way of accessing fantasy material (at all three topographical levels, conscious, preconscious, and unconscious), our focused bimodal approach which we will explicate below, offers a more directive focus in utilizing fantasy in treatment. Indeed, this bimodal approach focuses on sexual fantasy as a bridge that both links the cognitive-behavioral and psychodynamic components and serves as an organizing schemata for treatment intervention.

BIMODAL APPROACH TO TREATMENT

As mentioned above, the bimodal approach is a synthesis of two basic treatment modalities: the cognitive-behavioral and the psychodynamic. The domain of cognitive-behavioral techniques applies to the accessible, conscious fantasy, or the overt behavior. Cognitive-behavioral techniques, as applied to paraphiliacs, are especially important in their emphasis on the individual rapidly gaining self-control of his deviant sexual behavior. Psychodynamic methodology, on the other hand, is oriented toward achieving insight into the meaning of the unconscious features of the symptomatic behavior. This in-depth understanding may contribute to the patient's development of increased control over his behavior. The reluctance of some therapists to use psychodynamic therapies with compulsive paraphiliacs derives from the fact that, unlike cognitive-behavioral technologies, psychodynamic therapies do not emphasize the spectrum of monitoring techniques that are oriented toward extinguishing the target behaviors. When a more symptom-focused psychodynamic methodology can be integrated with a more target-focused cognitive-behavioral methodology, the two modalities can act so as to complement one another, thus bringing about the amelioration of deviant symptomatology. As Wachtel[6] has noted, in integrating psychodynamic with behavioral therapies in the treatment of a wide range of clinical disorders, alteration in overt behaviors can result in changes in insight and self-image; also, increased understanding of unconscious processes, that is, motivations, defenses, and relational patterns, can result in changes in overt behavior. This reciprocal interaction of the two modalities, which addresses both the conscious and unconscious aspects of the sexual perversion, can have a synergistic therapeutic impact on the patient. In effect, external behavioral changes can promote internal changes, just as internal changes can promote external behavioral changes.

COGNITIVE-BEHAVIORAL COMPONENT

Cognitive-behavioral methodologies are useful in treating virtually the whole array of deviant sexual disorders. The way these methodologies are incorporated in treatment depends upon a host of patient-centered and treatment-context factors. In the treatment of severe sex offenders, that is, acting-out pedophiles, we recommend using the complete cognitive-behavioral protocol, particularly those elements that focus on self-control. Thus, techniques including relapse prevention approaches, covert sensitization, and/or masturbatory satiation are clearly indicated. Especially important in this protocol is the continual monitoring of the patient's potential for acting out, and of the degree to which the patient has been responding to treatment. The elicitation of conscious fantasy production and evaluation of its intensity allow us to estimate the degree of the patient's self control. This estimate can be arrived at via a variety of self-report measures and can be assisted by penile plethysmographic studies. We ask the patient to monitor the frequency of his deviant sexual fantasies and to report this on a periodic basis. Many individuals with severe paraphilias suffer from a variety of social-interpersonal deficits; consequently, after the patient has gained sufficient control over his deviant fantasies, urges, and/or potential for acting out, we recommend that he participate in such treatment modalities as stress management, assertiveness training, and social-communicative skills training. It should be pointed out that these severe sex offender patients are involved with the criminal justice system; therefore, though an experienced, individual practitioner may provide such treatment, these patients are often treated in special treatment programs.

In the treatment of the moderately disordered paraphiliac individual, that is, the individual who has in the past acted in a deviant sexual manner but does not have the degree of repetitiveness and compulsivity that marks the severely disordered paraphiliac, we recommend a more flexible approach to the utilization of cognitive-behavioral techniques. A case example is an exhibitionist who was apprehended for his activity and who now is in better control but periodically experiences fantasies and urges. Another example is a sexual masochist who periodically acts on his fantasies by going to prostitutes. Therapists adopting this more selective utilization of cognitive-behavioral interventions should not, though, minimize the importance of relapse prevention and the need to be continuously sensitive to the risk factors in the cognitive-behavioral chain of events comprising the patterns of experience and behavior that culminate in the deviant sexual act. In conjunction with relapse-prevention techniques, we also recommend the judicious use of stress-management techniques in order to help the individual to better cope with troubling affective states that might otherwise contribute or even lead to the patient's perverse sexual behavior.

In the treatment of the mildly disordered paraphiliac patient, that is, the individual who has never acted out but who periodically experiences distressing, sexually perverse fantasies, we recommend timely and selective cognitive-behavioral techniques. Obviously, if the patient reports an escalation in the frequency and intensity of his conscious, distressing fantasies and urges, the clinician should increase the use of cognitive-behavioral interventions.

FOCUSED PSYCHODYNAMIC COMPONENT

In contrast to psychoanalytic therapy, the focused psychodynamic therapy approach is more active, directive, and focused on the specific presenting symptomatology, ie, sexually perverse behavior. Focused psychodynamic therapy is consistent with the current trend toward brief dynamic psychotherapy, an approach first articulated in the early psychoanalytic works of Ferenczi[7] and Rank,[8] and more recently elaborated on in the writings of Malan,[9] Balint,[10] Sifneos,[11] Davanloo,[12] and Horowitz.[13] These therapists represent uncovering approaches focused on core conflicts and defenses. These approaches are sometimes used for specific symptomatic problems.

The prominent work in this form of psychotherapy consists of helping the patients gain insight into the meaning, purpose, and etiologic significance of the motivating perverse fantasy that has served as an organizing themata in the patient's sexual life. In this treatment modality, the therapist gains access into the patient's unconscious fantasy life by elucidating the patient's conscious fantasy productions. The therapist treats the patient's conscious fantasy and ritualized acting out as a kind of manifest dream content that initiates the inquiry into the unconscious elements of the compulsive deviant sexuality. The conscious sexual fantasy serves as a kind of "leitmotif" throughout the sessions of the treatment. Depending upon the process flow of the session, it can be emphasized and referred to by the therapist in order to achieve the goal of arriving at a comprehensive understanding of the nature, purpose, function, and meaning of the patient's perverse sexuality. An exploration directed so as to access memories, affects, interpersonal integrations, and defensive operations intrinsic to the perverse sexual act is central to the dynamic basis of treatment. The attempt to connect the patient's contemporary experiences with important episodes in the patient's past, particularly those episodes and experiences related to traumatogenic sexual events, is of primary importance. The purpose of this is to foster an awareness on the part of the patient that current stresses contribute to the upsurge of earlier unresolved conflicts and hence create a pressure to "concretize" the symptom by acting it out. With the use of this uncovering technique, a clearer understanding of the unconscious meaning of the patient's sexual disorder emerges, a meaning which forms the underpinning of the presentation of the patient's conscious fantasy material. A variety of heuristic interpretive strategies of a dynamic nature which can be utilized by the therapist are discussed in Chapter 6 (this volume);

here, it is necessary to reiterate only our conviction that, whatever interpretive approach is used, it must be experienced as "near," and should stay close to the patient's lived experiences. As in most psychodynamic therapies, the process unfolds essentially through confrontation clarification, interpretation, and working through.[14] The therapist helps the patient explore the dynamic significance of the stresses and affective states—particularly those that involve object losses and narcissistic injuries—that appear to precipitate fantasy production and sexually perverse activity. By consistently working through these psychological patterns, the patient's sense of ego control over the fantasy can be enhanced. This process, in turn, can contribute to the reinforcement of the patient's ego structure.

MULTIMODAL INTEGRATION

Although we advocate the core bimodal approach described above, an approach comprising a synthesis of the cognitive-behavioral and focused psychodynamic components, as an applicable and efficacious approach for the majority of sexually perverse patients, we also recognize the appropriateness of integrating other modalities, which we described earlier, including organic, family systems, and also longer-term psychodynamic approaches. We should also point out what would seem to be the obvious, but nonetheless merits mention: the sexually perverse individual often has a variety of problems that arise during treatment, and he may be suffering from long-standing characterological deficits. A common feature is that patients enter treatment with varying degrees of depression subsequent to the disclosure of their sexual problem. This has to be taken into consideration in the application of an integrated treatment modality. In some severe cases of depression, we recommend an antidepressant medication, particularly Prozac, which, as noted above, has been reported in preliminary studies as beneficial in the treatment of some paraphiliac disorders. In any case, a guiding principle of the bimodal synthesis (cognitive-behavioral and psychodynamic) is that the therapist must make an initial determination of the patient's control over his sexually perverse symptomatology. In addition, the therapist should make an estimate of the patient's psychological-minded capacity to undergo a more introspective experience. Basically, there is no one mechanical approach that can be applied across the board for all patients. The bimodal application depends necessarily on the nature of the therapeutic alliance. This bimodal approach can be adapted for treatment durations of brief to moderate periods from one to two years, as well as for long-term treatment of beyond two years. Naturally, the latter treatment modality would probably utilize psychoanalytically oriented approaches.

REFERENCES

1. Protter B, Travin S. Sexual fantasies in the treatment of paraphiliac disorders: a bimodal approach. *Psyhiatr Q.* 1987;58:279–297.
2. Abel GG, Blanchard EB. The role of fantasy in the treatment of sexual deviation. *Arch Gen Psychiatry.* 1974;30:467–475.
3. Meichenbaum DH. *Cognitive-Behavior Modification: An Integrative Approach.* New York, NY: Plenum Press; 1977.
4. Mendelsohn E, Silverman LH. The activation of unconscious fantasies in behavioral treatments. In: Arkowitz H, Messer, SB, eds. *Psychoanalytic Therapy and Behavior Therapy: Is Integration Possible?* New York, NY: Plenum Press; 1984.
5. Messer SN. Behavioral and psychoanalytic perspectives at therapeutic choice points. *Amer Psychol.* 1986;41:1261–1272.
6. Wachtel PL. *Psychoanalysis and Behavior Therapy: Toward an Integration.* New York, NY: Basic Book; 1977.
7. Ferenczi S. The further development of active therapy in psychoanalysis. In: Rickman J, ed. *Further Contributions to the Theory and Techniques of Psychoanalysis.* London, England: Hogarth Press; 1950.
8. Rank O. *Will Therapy.* New York, NY: Knopf; 1947.
9. Malan DH. *Frontiers of Brief Psychotherapy.* New York, NY: Plenum Press; 1976.
10. Balint M, Ornstein PH, Balint E. *Focal Psychotherapy.* Philadelphia, Pa: JB Lippincott; 1972.
11. Sifneos PE. *Short-Term Psychotherapy: Evaluation and Technique.* New York, NY: Plenum Press; 1979.
12. Davanloo H, ed. *Short-Term Dynamic Therapy, I.* New York, NY: Jason Aronson; 1980.
13. Horowitz M, Marmar C, Krupnick J, Wilner N, Kaltreider N, Wallerstein R. *Personality Styles and Brief Psychotherapy.* New York, NY: Basic Books Inc; 1984.
14. Bibring E. Psychoanalysis and the dynamic psychotherapies. *J Amer Psychoanal Assoc.* 1954;2:745–770.

10

Clinical Applications of Treatment
Integrative Approaches

Sexual perversion, as has been discussed throughout this book, is not a unitary phenomenon. It manifests itself in many varieties and degrees of severity. The most crucial distinction from the point of view of treatment is between those perversions that actively present a danger to potential victims and those perversions that are less threatening to other individuals. The former patients are more likely to be referred for treatment through the criminal justice system, whereas the latter are usually referred through more traditional sources of referral in which the presenting complaints may not necessarily be the sexual problem. This referral distinction may not always be operative. That is, the therapist during the course of treatment may discover that the patient is experiencing severe fantasies or urges that are potentially threatening to others, or worse, he is acting on them.

Because of the complexity of sexual perversion and the differences in treatment context, we conceptualize a variety of sexually perverse patients that vary according to patient type and setting. These categories of patients will be discussed in case illustrations. These cases have been altered to preserve anonymity; aspects of them represent composites seen either by the authors or supervisees of the authors. It is important to point out that these categorizations, which roughly conform to the DSM-III-R categories of severity in paraphiliac disorder, can only be approximations of severity because evaluation of the paraphiliac activity is largely based on self-reports, corroborating police or probationary records, and ancillary psychological and physiological assessment procedures. All of these methodologies clearly have limitations in validity.

As mentioned above, our treatment approach is centered around a core bimodal (cognitive-behavioral and psychodynamic) framework. However, we are flexible in our approach to incorporate ancillary treatment modalities as needed.

1. *The severe paraphiliac patient*—setting of treatment:
    (a) specialized program—Case 1
    (b) private practice referral—Case 2
    (c) disclosure in psychotherapy—Case 3
2. *The moderate paraphiliac patient*—setting of treatment:
    (a) specialized program
    (b) private practice referral
    (c) disclosure in psychotherapy—Case 4 and Case 5
3. *The mild paraphiliac patient*—setting of treatment:
    (a) private practice referral
    (b) disclosure in psychotherapy—Case 6
4. *The transient sexually perverse experience*—setting of treatment:
    (a) disclosure in psychotherapy—clinical vignette
5. *The compulsive nonparaphiliac sexually disordered patient*—setting of treatment:
    (a) disclosure in psychotherapy—clinical example
    (b) private practice referral for cross-addictions
    (c) self-help programs
6. *Female sexual perversions*

THE SEVERE PARAPHILIAC PATIENT

According to the DSM-III-R, a severe paraphiliac means that "the person has repeatedly acted on the paraphilic urge" (p 281). Severe paraphiliacs who become patients have mostly been referred by the criminal justice system to court-related specialized treatment programs, especially to the group therapy format. In recent years, there have been an increasing number of private practitioners who consider many of these patients to be treatable, consistent with the current trend in treating other specific populations such as acting-out addictive disorders and borderline conditions. It is important to note, however, that virtually none of these severe paraphiliac patients are self-referred, that is, willing to seek out treatment without any third-party coercion. There are probably three basic reasons for this lack of self-motivation: (1) the ego-syntonic pleasurable nature of many of these disorders; (2) the profound shame in disclosure; and (3) the real possibility that the psychotherapist will report the unlawful activity. Additionally, psychotherapists should be aware that although the patient may have entered treatment for other complaining symptoms, he may, during the course of treatment, with increasing trust in the psychotherapist, reveal a severe paraphiliac problem.

Specialized Treatment Program

In general, specialized treatment programs follow a well-established treatment protocol, with both inclusionary and exclusionary criteria for admission into the program. The treatment modality is usually in the group format. Close collaboration with the criminal justice system (probation or parole) is maintained, as well as an emphasis on relapse prevention measures. The patient signs a detailed informed consent in which he agrees to adhere to a structured assessment and treatment protocol.

Case 1. Pedophilia, Same Sex

Mr A is a 34-year-old single, unemployed male who as a condition of parole was referred by the Parole Department to a specialized court-related program for the treatment of male pedophilia. He had served five years in a state prison after being convicted of sodomizing two small boys between the ages of 5 and 7 years. While in prison, he sporadically attended a counseling group for sex offenders.

During the initial assessment phase, Mr A tended to minimize his sexual activity with young boys, claiming he had befriended them and on occasion merely fondled them. He agreed to undergo the complete assessment protocol, and though he felt he no longer had a sexual problem, he would accept treatment if the therapists felt he needed it. His sexual and social histories revealed an isolative pattern with a great deal of time spent with young boys, especially in his various roles as camp counselor and youth activity leader. Although he reluctantly acknowledged having some erotic fantasy material toward young boys, the interviewers had a distinct impression that he gave inconsistent accounts of these experiences and was not fully disclosing them. Penile plethysmographic studies showed high arousal to young boys and some mild violent propensities. The evaluators felt that the patient had minimal insight and psychological mindedness and determined that he had a serious pedophilic problem that required immediate intervention. When confronted with the assessment, the patient agreed to undergo treatment. The patient was placed in cognitive-behavioral–oriented group therapy. The most immediate task was to assure control of his deviant sexuality. In this first phase of group therapy, group members were educated about their individual risk factors as an introduction to relapse prevention. Mr A agreed as a condition of continued treatment to refrain from any activities that placed him alone with small boys. Then the group was introduced into two self-control cognitive-behavioral tasks: covert sensitization and masturbatory satiation. A follow-up penile plethysmographic study revealed that the patient's arousal pattern to small boys was markedly reduced.

Because of his apparent poor self-esteem, mild depressive and relational difficulties, the therapists felt that he could benefit from short-term supportive-expressive individual psychotherapy that dynamically focused on underlying characterological issues. Specifically, the patient had himself been sexually victimized by a family member when he was a child. It was apparent that his deviant sexuality was, in part, an enactment of repressed rageful feelings. Although the patient's insight was somewhat limited, he was able to gain some understanding into the sources of his sexual problem. Moreover, the individual psychotherapy proved to be a valuable supplement to the group because it reinforced for the individual a fuller sense of himself as a person having a unique set of psychodynamics.

Following the two self-control tasks, the group was engaged in a variety of social-rehabilitative activities, that is, social skills, assertiveness training, and cognitive restructuring exercises and sexual education. This phase of treatment lasted approximately one year, and then the patients were assigned to an ongoing relapse-prevention group.

Private Practice Referral

An important distinction can be made between the specialist in this area who treats a great many of these kinds of patients and the general mental health clinician who may be somewhat knowledgeable but does not usually treat these patients. The specialist may therefore have a greater latitude in offering individual and/or group therapy, whereas, the latter clinician, who may see only an occasional paraphiliac patient, can likely only offer informed individual treatment. Thus, the general practitioner should be able to assess the needs of the individual patient and be prepared to refer the patient to a specialist in this area. The general practitioner, who is deciding whether or not to refer a severe paraphiliac patient, should be cognizant of the specialized assessment techniques, forensic-related considerations (eg, double agentry, limitations of confidentiality, and third-party liability), as well as the extant specialized treatment techniques.

Case 2. Pedophilia, Opposite Sex, Incest

Mr B is a 39-year-old male employed as an accountant in a large corporation, whose wife had demanded that he leave her and their two children after their 12-year-old daughter informed her mother that he had been having sexual relations with this child. Mrs B had contacted the child protective services and the case came to the attention of Family Court. Mr B was arrested and briefly jailed. As a condition of probation he was mandated to undergo psychiatric treatment for his deviant sexual problem. The rest of the family was also referred for treatment with another therapist.

Mr B chose to undergo private treatment with a clinician who specialized in the treatment of sexual disorders, which met the requirements for mandated treatment. Mr B did not deny the charge that he had been having sexual intercourse with his 12-year-old daughter, but he initially claimed that it only happened three times in the past year. Furthermore, he insisted that his daughter had been acting seductively toward him and seemed to have enjoyed this physical relationship. Although at times he had experienced some guilt about this sexual relationship, the perception that his daughter seemed to look forward to the physical expression of his love for her, served to reduce the intensity of his guilt feelings. Moreover, he described his wife as "frigid" to him and indifferent to the daughter. He also described his having been under intense stress at work during the past year.

In addition to performing the standard initial psychiatric interviews, which obtained the above information, the therapist conducted a comprehensive sexual history, administered a number of psychometric testing instruments, including the Sexual Interest Card-Sort, Pedophile Cognition Scale, Assault Knowledge Inventory, and the Derogatis Sexual Functioning Inventory. These assessment instruments gave ambiguous indications of a mild sexual interest in young females. The patient insisted, however, that although he had experienced occasional sexual fantasies about young females, he had never acted on these fantasies or urges outside of his own family. The therapist recommended that the patient also undergo penile plethysmographic studies, but he refused. In light of the fact that the patient clinically did not appear to be an imminent threat of sexually acting out, the therapist decided to postpone a confrontation on the matter pending further clinical intervention.

The sexual history revealed that the patient's mother had been overly seductive to him when he was a child. He recalled a variety of instances in which his mother would comfort him in a sexualized manner, including spending an inordinate amount of time in bed with him, bathing him until the age of twelve, and walking around the house partially clad. She would constantly inquire about and intrude into his relationships with his peers. In the family system, he had become in effect, "triangulated," assuming the role of the little man-husband. He was an only child, and his father was frequently away on business trips. His father came across in the patient's description as a distant, shadowy, and indifferent figure. The patient suspects that his father had engaged in extramarital affairs. Until only recently his mother used to send him romanticized Valentine Day cards. In the past year, the patient learned for the first time that his mother had been sexually molested by her father, the patient's grandfather. At age 20, while working as a counselor in a children's summer camp, he began to have sexual fantasies about some of the young female campers. This disturbed him greatly, but he was able to suppress these kinds of fantasies, which would recur infrequently over the years, and only when he was under a great deal of stress. At age 26, shortly after graduating from accounting school, he married a 19-year-old, young-looking female who was a high-school graduate and employed as a secretary in his firm. During the course of the 13-year-long marriage, the couple twice sought marital counseling because of their lack of communication and sexual apathy on her part. He also complained about her nagging, overbearing, and intruding qualities. The patient was clearly articulate and demonstrated a high degree of psychological-mindedness and capacity to acquire psychological awareness of his difficulties. In view of these insightful capacities, the patient's request for individual treatment rather than group therapy was deemed worthy of a therapeutic trial. The therapist reasoned that depending upon the process of individual treatment, alterations could be made accordingly.

It should be pointed out again here that in the bimodal approach, with patients who are not in good control and at risk to act out sexually, self-control techniques, particularly those of covert sensitization and masturbatory satiation, are usually initiated immediately. Subsequent to the patient gaining this control, the therapist begins the focused psychodynamic-therapy part of the bimodal approach. In the case of Mr B, the two components—cognitive-behavioral and psychodynamic—were initiated simultaneously. We also emphasize that the patient was cautioned about the inherent risk factors of being alone with his daughters, or for that matter, with any young female.

Initially, the cognitive-behavioral tasks concentrated on utilizing narratives of events and experiences combined with conscious fantasy material. In covert sensitization, the patient constructed a chain of events and internal experiences, including affective mental states, felt impressions, sensations and fantasy-laden material that would escalate in a linkage leading to the deviant sexual activity. The patient described a typical scenario of coming home from work with mild dysphoria and low self-esteem, usually as a residue from feelings of being underappreciated for his efforts at work (mostly related to his supervision by a domineering supervisor). These mild dysphoric feelings were usually exacerbated by a typically cool, criticizing, and rejecting attitude by his wife. This in turn would cause Mr B to become angry and verbally abusive with accompanying thoughts that this "stupid bitch will never understand me." He would then go into a kind of numb and withdrawn state with fantasies of fondling and cuddling his older daughter while thinking "she is the only thing that makes it bearable." Typically, his wife retires to bed earlier than he does, which gives him time to enter his daughter's bedroom alone. After he wakes her up, she asks him how his day at work went, and she kisses him. The patient interprets this as an indication of desire on the part of his daughter for further physical contact. Although, typically, Mr B would then begin to fondle his daughter's breasts prior to sexual intercourse, he instead switches to a self-constructed aversive scene applicable to his own life circumstances as part of this cognitive-behavioral task. The aversive scene that Mr B constructs is that the police are arriving at his home, arresting and handcuffing him while his wife is screaming at him and his daughters are crying. The covert sensitization task continued for a period of six weeks.

In masturbatory satiation, Mr B constructed a hierarchy in descending order of pleasurable sexual experiences that he had with his daughter. Foremost of the experiences was sexual intercourse followed by cunnilingus, fondling her vagina, her breasts, and then deep kissing. While talking into a tape recorder, Mr B would masturbate while fantasizing about a normal consensual sexual scene with an adult for 10 minutes or until ejaculation. Then he would continue masturbating to the point of satiation while fantasizing about having sexual intercourse with his daughter, emphasizing that he is 39 years of age and his daughter is 12 years old. Each of these hierarchic scenes of deviant sexual fantasy continues for approximately 10 minutes. The entire tape therefore ran for one hour. Similar to covert sensitization, masturbatory satiation continued for six weeks.

Psychodynamic therapy proceeded from a discussion of the sexual material closest to the surface presentation to an unfolding of the more underlying meaning of the deviant sexuality. The immediate reference points of the deviant sexual behavior, which provided a linkage between the cognitive-behavioral approach and the psychodynamic methodology, were the structured events (chain of external and internal experiences) which the patient presented in the covert sensitization procedure. This description of events in the chain leading up to the sexual act provided a working paradigm from which the therapist made inquires into the topographical meanings—conscious, preconscious, and unconscious—of the perverse sexuality. In essence, this chain of encapsulated experiences served as a kind of primary source material, much like the manifest content of a repetitive dream from which manifold latent meaning can be elicited. During the course of treatment, the therapist repeatedly focused on this material as a "leitmotif" for further elaboration.

The initial focus was to facilitate the patient's capacity to articulate as clearly as possible the nuances of his subjectively affect-laden states that accompany the narrational sequence of events culminating in the sexualization of his experiences. A "second" order of the sequence of events can be schematized as follows: indifference and underappreciation on the part of his boss elicit in him feelings of frustration, helplessness, anger, self-depreciation, and low self-esteem. At home, the carping, demanding, and rejecting attitude of his wife intensifies his feelings of rage and dysphoria. This inchoate brew of unsettling affective tensions continues to escalate to the point where he feels compelled to obtain some kind of relief/release. It is then that he begins to think and fantasize about his daughter. These ideational contents, which are rapidly sexualized, are abetted by the cognitive distortion that his daughter's responsiveness is her desire for a sexual union. Thus, the therapist delineated with the patient what was hitherto a confused jumble of feelings into a more clearly articulated sequence of identified affective states that become transformed into perverse sexuality. At this juncture, the therapist introduced cognitive-behavioral exercises on assertiveness and social/communication skills training to help the patient cope better with dysfunctional interpersonal behavior while also continuing exploration of psychodynamic issues. In psychodynamic therapy, with directed inquiry, the patient began to discuss in considerable detail the meanings he attributed to his masturbatory fantasies and sexual experiences. As the atmosphere of safety improved for him in therapy, the patient disclosed for the first time that he had been sexually fondling his daughter for a period of two years, even before he had engaged in sexual intercourse with her. After this disclosure he was able to talk more freely and recount more clearly memories concerning his own rather sexualized experiences with his mother. Of particular note was his description of what seemed to touch on gender dysphoric issues, namely episodes in his mid-teens of dressing in his mother's undergarments while masturbating to fantasies of being fellated by a strong male figure. On some occasions he would look in the mirror and get sexually aroused by the sight of his own erection and proceed to masturbate with the above fantasy. He related that at such times he simultaneously felt that he was both a man and a woman.

In the process of eliciting this enriched flow of dynamic material, the therapist reintroduced aspects of the "primary" chain, particularly the fantasy of securing sexual comfort from his daughter. The patient was now more able to make associative linkages of this fantasy to his own sexually tinged childhood experiences with his mother. He began to remember hitherto repressed feelings of being comforted, yet somehow uneasy, and even sometimes repulsed, by his mother's physical ministrations. He seemed to remember that these experiences with his mother would usually occur while his father was away. The patient was also able to connect some of his repressed feelings about his unavailable father with his current feelings toward his supervisor.

By the end of the first year of treatment the patient began to work with the therapist on deeper levels of unconscious material wherein psychogenetic interpretations could be considered. The therapist was able to facilitate the patient's associative linkages

Clinical Applications of Treatment

into these deeper levels by the therapist continually reintroducing the patient's conscious fantasies of the "primary" chain, that is, anger and frustration in his work life, rejection and fury toward his wife, and sexualized consolation from his daughter. In this continuing uncovering analytic process, the therapist was able to assist the patient in gaining a clearer understanding of the unconscious meaning of his conscious sexual fantasies. In essence, the patient's unconscious fantasy material had multiple roots and was completely layered in his psychic life, which ultimately emerged in the concretization of his sexual symptom. This overdetermined sexual symptom was best understood from a pluralistic perspective that drew upon a variety of classical and relational-oriented theories. What psychodynamically emerged was a picture of a young boy whose castration anxiety had been intensified by the compensatory sexualized bonding of an unhappy and frustrated mother angered at her distant and unavailable husband. This sexualized bonding with his mother served to intensify his imagined fear of a retaliatory father and contributed toward his gender dysphoric feelings as he clung more tenaciously to his mother for consolation and protection. His clinging to his mother increasingly led to a closer, yet anxiously ambivalent identification with her. The therapist suggested that the patient's mother, who herself had been sexually abused as a child, had probably initiated her sexualized connection with the infant at a very early age because of her own emotional needs. The therapist helped the patient understand that his various early masturbatory rituals, such as wearing his mother's clothes and his fantasizing assuming a female role, as well as his erotic stimulation in viewing his erection in the mirror, were manifestations of a need to reassure his sense of masculinity. Additionally, these masturbatory rituals served the purpose of consoling him during the periods of his attempts to separate from his needy and clinging mother. The therapist emphasized that the patient had undoubtedly experienced a difficult and unresolved individuation-separation developmental process. Indeed, this separation-individuation struggle was still an ongoing dynamic in himself. In his current life situation, there appeared to be a number of reenactments of these earliest dynamic themes. His troublesome experiences with his supervisor at work had analogs with his distant, unavailable, and feared father. His relationship with his wife and daughter appeared to be a result of a splitting operation between two aspects of his incorporated mother, from whom he was never adequately able to psychically separate. Thus, the rejecting wife represented the "bad," controlling, and devouring mother, and the daughter represented the "good," consoling mother to whom he was still pathologically attached. In addition, a role reversal would occur, wherein he would maintain his identification with his mother by sexualizing his relationship with his daughter as his own mother had done with him. Moreover, this sexual relationship with his daughter served as an outlet for his retaliatory aggression against his mother toward whom he harbored a great deal of unconscious rage.

Disclosure in Psychotherapy

Case 3. Sexual Masochism

Mr C was a 41-year-old married man, father of two small children, owner of a copying-printing shop, who came into psychotherapeutic treatment at the urging of his wife because of her concerns about his reported gambling and episodic cocaine usage and deteriorating marital relationship. She had seriously threatened to leave him. Mr C started his treatment as twice-a-week psychotherapy sessions, and he agreed, when circumstances warranted it, that his wife would be invited in for couple's therapy. Mr C was a mild-mannered, fastidious, passive, and conscientious man. He stated that he had gone into business to avoid the rigid routine of employment in a large corporation, and that he cherished the independence of his own time. Mr C was somewhat vague about the extent of his gambling problem, but he said he was determined to stop it. He also acknowledged that he snorted cocaine approximately once or twice a week, a problem which he also wanted help in controlling. The therapist directed his therapeutic intervention toward both of these presenting problems, as well as the underlying interfactional difficulties with his wife. His wife participated in several adjunctive couple's sessions.

The individual therapy went on for about five months and focused on his presenting problems and marital difficulties. There was considerable exploration directed toward his own difficult relationship with a domineering and shrewlike mother. He had been an only child, and his father had died of a heart attack when the patient was 5 years old. He described the situation with his mother when he was a child and throughout his life, as being overly controlled like a "spider caught in a web." Yet his feelings were markedly ambivalent toward her. The therapist began to view the patient's gambling and cocaine usage as a kind of ecstatic escape from his sense of being imprisoned within himself. After several months, Mr C claimed to have stopped the gambling and cocaine abuse. Despite this improvement, the therapist felt that the sessions were permeated by a certain quality of guardedness in his disclosing more intimate aspects of his life, particularly in the sexual area. Indeed, the therapist at this point felt that he was speaking to a "good" patient, but did not really know him as a person.

In the ninth month of treatment, Mr C came in for his usual session in an extremely anxious condition. He stated that he was thinking of dropping out of treatment because his business was doing poorly and he could no longer afford the expense. His wife had moved out of the house and was staying with her mother. She had discovered that there were thousands of dollars missing from their joint savings account. Upon further inquiry, he acknowledged that in the past month he had reverted to his cocaine habit. When confronted by the therapist as to why he had not reported this situation sooner, the patient suddenly broke down to tears and became extremely ashamed. He blurted out that he had spent most of the missing money on high-priced prostitutes whom he had engaged for sadomasochistic practices in conjunction with abusing cocaine.

Mr C then disclosed that he has had a sexual preoccupation of a masochistic nature for much of his adult life. During the next several sessions he proceeded to disclose in a shameful and embarrassed tone considerable details about his sexual perversion. He described his overwhelming need at times to be physically whipped, urinated on, tied up, and verbally humiliated by a dominant woman in spiked heels and wearing black leather garments. During these sexual encounters he himself would often be wearing diapers. Periodically, he would go on a two-months' binge visiting these dominatrix prostitutes as often as three times a week. This sexual preoccupation over the years had been costing him a small fortune, but he felt irresistibly compelled to partake in what he considered to be his "double" life. Indeed, this was the first time he had ever told anybody about it, and he pleaded with the therapist not to reveal it to his wife. He did state that after many years of this compulsive behavior he wanted to stop it, and he recognized that this sexual perversion was jeopardizing both his marriage and his business. He understood that although he would occasionally gamble, this was just a pretext to account for the loss of money. The real issue was his compulsive deviant sexuality that was accompanied by occasional cocaine usage.

As a result of this dramatic disclosure, the treatment plan was altered. The first focus of treatment was to elicit the nature of the primary chain of behavior leading to the deviant sexuality. This consisted of stressful, overwhelming feelings at work leading to a decrement of self-esteem accompanied by severe self-accusations of inadequacy, a build-up of fantasized scenes of being physically and emotionally abused by a domineering woman, telephoning the brothel for an available appointment, and then actually going there. Treatment then proceeded simultaneously along three lines with varying degrees of emphasis depending upon the unfolding therapeutic process. These three lines were the self-control measures of covert sensitization, stress management, and focused psychodynamic therapy. Covert sensitization, which paired the chain with personal aversive scenes in the patient's life, was utilized as a tool to help the patient gain control over his impulse. Stress-management techniques, including the use of stress inoculation and cognitive interventions, were used to help the patient more effectively manage anxiety and stress, particularly in his work life. Of increasing significance then was the exploration of the specific psychodynamic issues relevant to his sexually deviant disorder, that is, sexual masochism. Due to the patient's sexually pathologic relationship with domineering women, the therapist felt it would be useful to explore in a focused manner the nature of the patient's early relationship with his mother. What emerged was a mother–son relationship marked by incessant, demanding expectations that the son continually act in ways developmentally beyond his chronological age in the service of taking care of the mother's needs. In effect, the son was placed in the role of a "spousified" child, constantly belittled, since he never lived up to the role, and he felt consequently enraged but unable to express his feelings because of fears of abandonment and retaliation by the mother. Many of these feelings lay buried in his unconscious and only became clear to him during the therapeutic process. It became apparent that the repetitive sexual acting out, that is, sexual masochism, represented an amalgam of psychodynamic themes, comprising classical, relational, and self psychological motifs. Within the classical framework, the patient's oedipal stage was confounded both by the mother's substituting for the father in her particularly controlling (ie, castrating) manner, and by the son's expected role of replacing the father (oedipal triumph), resulting in an intensification of unconscious oedipal guilt. This oedipal guilt may be derivative of the need for pain as a requirement for pleasure. From a relational perspective, the patient had never effectively separated from his maternal introject (because of the traumatogenic nature of the relationship) and had, in fact, incorporated this construct into a perverse scene that he continually and compulsively reenacted. In effect, the sexually masochistic scenario is a replication of a hurtful affective relationship. The pain that was once inflicted upon him (by his mother) is now transformed by the perverse act into a pleasurable victory. In some way the perversion serves to maintain the connection with the mother. But this repetitive connection (with a faulty maternal introject) can only provide temporary relief from fragmented, unsettling self states, and can never repair the deficient internal structures of the self, that maintain the ongoing sexual perversion. That is, following the short-lived gratification of the perverse act, the patient experiences increased shame, guilt, stress (due to fear of being found out and losing his family) that reinforce his dysphoric, fragmented sense of self. A vicious cycle thereby ensues. The therapist was increasingly able to be available as a humanizing agent to facilitate the patient the task of coping with these unsettling affects that had earlier propelled the perverse activity. As therapy proceeded, the patient was able to disclose more of his internal states, so that the therapy became more facilitative in containing his troubled affective life.

Later on, when more in control of his impulses and behavior, he agreed to have his wife returned for couple's therapy. Although he never disclosed to her the true extent of his sexual perversion, he did reveal his sexual dissatisfactions with his wife's passivity. This led to some improvement in their sexual relationship. Furthermore, his ability to control his spending on prostitutes improved his financial situation and reduced his overall stress.

THE MODERATE PARAPHILIAC PATIENT

The DSM-III-R describes a moderate paraphiliac as having "occasionally acted on the paraphiliac urge." Similar to severe paraphiliac individuals, these patients may be referred to specialized treatment programs, private practitioners, or seek treatment for a variety of other presenting problems.

Case 4. Exhibitionism and Voyeurism—
Disclosure in Psychotherapy

Mr D is a 34-year-old shoe salesman who was in treatment with a psychotherapist following his girlfriend's breaking up their 6-month-long relationship. He had sought treatment due to feelings of self-doubt about his ability to sustain a meaningful relationship that could lead to what he said was a desired marriage. Mr D had a long-standing difficulty in committing himself in relationships with females. His usual pattern, which was exemplified in this last relationship, was that just at the emotional point of a deepening closeness to his partner he would sabotage the relationship by distancing himself from her by various means such as his over-involvement with work and increasing criticism and fault-finding in her. Despite his self-defeating participation in this pattern of behavior, Mr D somehow experienced himself as a victim in these relational break-ups that reinforced his self-image of ineffectuality toward women. He described his early background as being the only child of an unhappy couple. The atmosphere in this home was both tense and lonely. His father was often away and he believed him to have engaged in a number of extramarital affairs. He perceived his mother as "icy" and undemonstrative. He felt ignored by his parents, unable to connect with them, and "as if I didn't exist there."

During the course of 4 months of dynamic psychotherapy, a variety of psychodynamic themes were explored. The psychotherapist placed particular emphasis on themes of conflicts in intimacy and the patient's sense of himself as undeserving of a relationship. The patient began to develop a good therapeutic alliance with the therapist and the nature of the transference was that of a mirroring-idealizing one. During the summer the therapist went on a 3-weeks' vacation. When the therapist returned, Mr D disclosed to the psychotherapist in a shaken tone of voice that he was fearful that he might be arrested for indecent exposure. He related that just prior to exiting the commuter railroad car, he exposed his erect penis to a female rider. When she looked away in disgust, he hurriedly ran out and spent the subsequent week in a state of near panic, fearful that he might encounter her again in the commuter train, and she would report him to the police. Mr D stated that he had already exhibited himself at the onset of treatment and approximately each time he had broken up a relationship with a woman. Upon further inquiry, he also acknowledged that he engaged at times in other types of compulsive sexuality, including voyeuristic fantasies and activities such as peeping into windows in his neighborhood and into the women's locker room at his health club. He also would go on bingelike activities at peep shows during some lunch hours while at work. Following these revelations the psychotherapist decided to refer the patient for treatment with one of the authors.

Initially, the specialist sought to determine the extent of the patient's control over his exhibitionistic and voyeuristic urges. The specialist conducted a detailed sexual history, administered several psychometric testings, and explored the patient's perceptions of sexual acting out. The specialist elicited two primary chains for his exhibitionistic and voyeuristic behaviors for covert sensitization. The key triggering factors in his primary chain centered on a constellation of anxieties, fears, and dysphoric states concerning his capacity to impact upon people, his inability to follow through in his relationships with others, and a general sense of hopelessness and inadequacies about himself. These perceived ineffectual states varied in their context from the work environment to social and interpersonal affairs and more intimate heterosexual relationships. In effect, many of his stresses were generated in the relational sphere. These stresses escalated into a chain of sequential experiences which culminated in the deviant sexual behavior. As such, these sequential escalating experiences constituted risk factors which the therapist was able to incorporate in the relapse-prevention aspect of treatment. By utilizing this chain in covert sensitization, the patient was able to understand more clearly how accelerating internal affective states that are intensified by his cognition (self-criticism, self-condemnation, and so forth) can rapidly become sexualized to the point where he is less able to control his actions. These actions then offer temporary mood-altering respite from the troubling internal states. The primary chains in covert sensitization served as a springboard for a focused dynamic inquiry into the meaning of his sexual acting out. Mr D reported no clear early sexual traumata in his past. He recounted that his first sexual experience was at age 10 and involved peeping through the keyhole in the bathroom of his aunt observing her urinating on the toilet. He vividly remembers being fascinated and sexually stimulated seeing her genital area. Subsequently, he began to episodically peep into neighbor's windows hoping to see nude females. At age 14, he recalled being in the boys' locker room at school overhearing someone mention that girls really liked boys who had large penises. Since he himself had sparse pubic hairs, no hair at all on his chest, and wondered if his penis was of an adequate size for his age, he began to be preoccupied about his physical development and worry whether or not he would develop like other boys. When he was 19 years old, and on a date with a girlfriend at a ballet performance, he remembered being startled by her comment that the leading male dancer had a large bulge in his genital area, which seemed to her to be quite sexy. This incident had a remarkable effect on him, and it seemed to confirm the notion that women could be sexually excited by the

Clinical Applications of Treatment 181

sight of men's genitalia. He began to have fantasies about exposing himself to women. Shortly afterward, he once undressed and exposed himself in front of his 11-year-old female cousin. His exhibitionistic behavior then generalized exclusively to adult females. Subsequent voyeuristic behavior was less frequent than the exhibitionistic behavior.

In the bimodal framework of therapy, the chain of internal experiences and affective states also served as a series of linkages to a host of associative memories and fantasies. This material served as an entry to preconscious and unconscious meanings of the sexual perversion by means of directed inquiry. Focused dynamic therapy brought to light the patients' sexual acting out as an overdetermined symptom. The symptomatic behavior encapsulated angry feelings toward women, whom he experienced as rendering him ineffectual and who represented to him shadowy and unreachable figures. His aloof and narcissistic mother was clearly the psychogenic analog for his perception of women. Simultaneously, the symptomatic acting out served to reaffirm that he had an impact upon women which he now concretized in a sexualized manner through the display of his erect penis. Furthermore, the symptom temporarily reaffirmed his sense of masculinity that was shaky due to an unavailable, insecure father who had spent considerable time during the patient's childhood having to prove his own sense of adequacy with women. A key theme that surfaced was the patient's sense of himself as a needy and ineffectual child who was never able to make an impact on others. His only male model was his burlesqued view of his father as an overmasculine "womanizing" man who made his mark on the world by transforming women into sexual objects. His deviant behavior can be seen as a collage of component aspects, including attempts to impact on an emotionally unavailable mother (female victim) and his identification with his father.

In this bimodal paradigm, the specialist continually employed the primary chains both as the means of eliciting affective states for the purposes of self-control and as the vehicles to gain access into preconscious and unconscious materials. The advantages of using these primary chains are that they help systematically organize for the patient experiences that are immediate, available on the surface, and have emotional impact. Consequently, preconscious and unconscious meaning connections reverberate for the patient as compelling and as a way to make sense of the sexual reenactment.

Case 5. Transvestic Fetishism—Disclosure in Psychotherapy

Mr E, a 30-year-old single, male attorney was referred for private psychotherapy because of anxiety seemingly related to his impending marriage to a woman he had been involved with for two years. Mr E attended psychodynamic-oriented psychotherapy on a twice-a-week basis. During the first few months, Mr E recounted a variety of anxieties he had concerning his job security at his law firm and more prominently ongoing doubts about his upcoming marriage, including whether he had made the right choice of a wife in a high-achieving woman, who is also an attorney. He claimed that he didn't want to wind up as did his own father, who was trapped in what he saw was an unsatisfactory marriage to his clinging, dependent, and hypochondriacal mother. He portrayed a picture of a family in which the father, as well as he and his older brother, were at the beck and call of his queenly mother, who always seemed to spend her time in doctors' offices or in bed with multiple complaints. About the fourth month into treatment, Mr E anxiously announced that he had not been totally candid about his real fears and reasons for coming to therapy. He then proceeded to describe an ongoing sexual preoccupation that had ebbed and flowed throughout the years. This preoccupation consisted of intense fantasies and urges of masturbating while rubbing and holding female underpants or stockings. On occasion he would put on female underpants and masturbate. Although he had for one year stopped acting on these urges, since he began dating his new fiancee, these urges had become more intense. In the past six months, roughly coinciding with his engagement to his fiancee, he had begun to masturbate frequently while rubbing and holding his fiancee's underpants and twice he put them on while masturbating. He was near panic that he could no longer control himself as he had been controlling himself fairly successfully for most of his life. He alternately worried that his fiancee would discover his problem and cancel their engagement, or that he himself should not marry because he might be some kind of "sick pervert." The patient stated he felt desperate and pleaded for help.

The therapist's first act was in providing reassurance that the present manifestation of the deviant sexuality was likely brought about by a variety of current anxieties that were surfacing in his life, particularly in relationship to his upcoming marriage. In addition, the therapist emphasized to the patient that he had been able to maintain control over his unusual sexual obsession for many years, and it was likely that this more intense involvement with his fiancee had stirred up anxieties that probably had contributed to the reestablishment of his earlier aberrant sexual pattern. Although the therapist's firm and supportive stance greatly reassured Mr E, the therapist added a more directive, cognitive-behavioral component to the treatment in order to help the patient gain control over his urges and behavior. The therapist began to instruct the patient on how to construct a chain of behaviors that lead up to the deviant sexual act as is utilized in covert sensitization. This helped the patient identify and monitor the behavioral cues and subjective experiences that culminate in his deviant sexual activity. The disclosure of the problem in therapy, the helpful reassurance on the part of the therapist, and the cognitive self-monitoring resulted in the patient's reporting of a decrement in his deviant urges. Both the therapist and the patient then agreed that the cognitive-behavioral self-control techniques would be used at a minimum, and the major focus of treatment would be to gain as clear as possible insight into the underlying meaning of the behavior relevant to this anxiety-laden relationship.

The psychodynamic formulation of the case could be summarized in the following way. The impending marriage had revived a variety of earlier conflicts and fears centering around such issues as dependency and gender identity, or his sense of masculinity, stemming from his conflicting identifications with both his mother and his father. The sexual acting out, in effect, was a symptomatic condensation representing many of these issues.

Historical data indicated that as a little boy, Mr E had an overly dependent relationship with his mother. Similar to his father, he had as a young boy been enlisted in a parentified manner in taking care of his mother. And he felt like his father did that whatever he did was insufficient to cure his mother's ailments. He developed a preoccupying concern that whenever he left her sick bed he was abandoning her, or she, in effect, would abandon him by dying. As the father retreated into his own work, the son was pushed increasingly into the role of a caretaker. By being drawn closer into his mother's orbit and sick bed, the father's significance diminished as an available figure for interaction and identification. Around the time of his first masturbatory activity at age 12, and while his mother was in the hospital undergoing one of her many medical workups, he began rubbing her undergarments while fantasizing being fondled by an older demonstrative woman. On one occasion he found himself masturbating while wearing his mother's underpants and stockings. He repeated this sexual activity and variation of it episodically throughout his adolescence. Although he was sexually inhibited and somewhat avoidant with his early female peers, starting in college he slowly began to develop a basically normal heterosexual dating pattern. During this phase of his life, his urges were much less frequent, although episodically his urges would arise for short and intense periods of activity.

Upon further inquiry, it became clear that Mr E had a host of anxieties and self-doubts about whether he could meet the needs of what he perceived about his fiancee as a woman who would expect too much of him. Would he be an adequate caretaker, or, for that matter, did he have deeply repressed longings to be taken care of himself? His current relationship with his fiancee had set into motion many of these previously repressed feelings. On a deeper level, the therapist explored the unconscious determinants of a pathological bond and identification with his mother. The symptomatic masturbatory activity represented both a wish to maintain the bond with his mother as well as an attempt to extricate himself from this union by the reassurance of his manhood via his sexual potency. The dynamic aspect of therapy continued with the therapist exploring with the patient these themes. The patient was subsequently able to marry and make a good heterosexual adjustment.

THE MILD PARAPHILIAC PATIENT

The DSM-III-R describes a mild paraphiliac as a person having periodic distressing urges and fantasies of a deviant nature without ever acting on them. In contrast to severe and moderate paraphilia, these patients do not act on their urges and fantasies and infringe on the rights of other persons. More than likely, these patients are encountered in psychotherapy where they may present with an array of other problems, such as anxiety, depression, and characterologic and relationship difficulties. It is probable that the patient may have harbored perverse fantasies for many years, although in some instances these fantasies may arise transiently due to increased stressful circumstances.

Case 6. The Sexually Masochistic Patient— Disclosure in Psychotherapy

Mr E, a 34-year-old single mental health professional, came to psychodynamic psychotherapy self-referred for mild characterological-related issues and for help to improve his relational life and career. He presented without a severe Axis-I–related problem, but his self-defeating and obsessional patterns prevented him from experiencing as much satisfaction in his life as he would like. He had some work inhibitions about achieving what he felt he could, and he had difficulty committing himself to one relationship.

About one month into treatment, Mr E revealed that he had been having an active sexual fantasy life since his early teenage years that was centered around themes of being humiliated by women. Although he frequently utilized these fantasies for masturbatory purposes, they would at times become distressing to him, particularly when they were clearly of an extreme nature. The earliest fantasies began during pubescence, when he would imagine himself being a slave to giant amazon women to be used at their beck and call. Later on the fantasies evolved into scenes in which large foreboding women would squat over him and urinate in his face while he imagined himself to be very small and helpless. At various times in his life he thought of engaging a prostitute to enact this scenario, but had felt too inhibited and ashamed to pursue it. Hence, he was confined to masturbating while fantasizing this scene, or on some occasions to buying pornographic material depicting this and related toilet scenes. On one occasion he summoned up enough courage to ask a girl he was briefly dating to carry out this fantasy, but she felt repulsed and refused. As a result, he never asked another female to do it. The fantasies seemed to increase in frequency at those times in which his self-esteem was lowest, often after a disappointment or perceived fear of rejection. On several occasions, while viewing film scenes of war and sadistic brutality, Mr E became extremely distressed to find that he was sexually aroused and experienced an erection.

Significant early background included an older sister, who had continually teased him about his small stature and shyness. His father was a rather crude and aggressive man, who was self-employed in the lady's garment industry. This father often belittled his son, minimizing his son's achievements and reproaching him for not amounting to anything. His mother was the only one who he felt genuinely understood him. He was mildly avoidant socially, started dating in college, but never had a steady girlfriend. He suffered from periodic episodes of mild depression and felt he was missing out in life by not becoming more fully involved with other people. From time to time he had thought of entering psychotherapy, and when one of his supervisors mentioned his own improvement in therapy, Mr E decided to follow suit.

During the course of further psychodynamic exploration, Mr E revealed that he engaged in frequent masturbatory deviant fantasies of being urinated upon and humiliated by women mostly when he was feeling lonely, disappointed, or down on himself; but, curiously, he had also the need to use these deviant fantasies during periods when he felt overly confident or buoyed up by success. This alternation of self-appraisal, which seemed to represent a fundamental aspect of his character, prevented him from achieving a balanced sense of self. As an example, when his supervisor at work would compliment him, Mr E would experience grandiose and unrealistic self-expectations, only to be subsequently followed by feelings of self-depreciation. These radical shifts in self-concept that somehow became connected with excessive deviant fantasies, contributed to Mr E's intense sense of imbalance in his life.

Psychodynamic psychotherapy of this mildly sexually perverse patient proceeded along the lines that were not different in substance from the psychodynamic treatment of any other symptomatic manifestation of characterological pathology. As such, the problems needed to be understood from the perspective of multipsychodynamic determinants. Khan's metaphor of the perverse scenario as a collage of meanings seems to be appropriate in this undertaking. As a corollary, the symptomatic relief of the sexual perversion cannot be attributed solely to the illumination of its underlying meanings. Symptomatic change needs to be understood as a function of a host of curative factors in the therapeutic process. Especially important is the corrective emotional experience in which the patient can test out new behaviors in the context of the therapeutic relationship.

Some of the more prominent psychodynamic themes that emerged during the course of treatment were the following. The picture of Mr E's background was that of a significantly dysfunctional family. Tyrannized by an autocratic, yet insecure father, the family essentially was divided along two lines of loyalty. The father's harshness, as well as his inability to be tender with or available as an idealizable, identifying figure to his son, increased the impact of his son's transition through the oedipal stage of development, thereby exacerbating inchoate experiences of castration anxiety. The older sister, allied and identified with the father, tended to reinforce the father's belittling, undermining, and humiliating effect on her younger brother. Mr E was able to recall hitherto repressed emotions of shame, inadequacy, self-loathing, and rage in response to both his father's and his sister's hurtful actions. As a result, Mr E continually sought comfort with his mother, who although overtly compliant and submissive to her husband, tried unsuccessfully to shield her son. Ultimately in treatment, Mr E began to recognize his repressed resentment of his mother's weakness in the face of his father's onslaughts. What became increasingly apparent was that the son has been essentially sacrificed by his mother for the purpose of her maintaining a secure attachment to her husband.

The deviant sexual fantasy represented a dramatic script that condensed important psychic elements derived from early family scenarios, with attempts at restitution. At the most manifest level, the fantasy of being urinated upon by women was a statement of his self-loathing, which was a product of early incorporated self-representations. Developmentally, the fantasy appeared to be a defense against castration anxiety and the traumata of an inadequate identification with a hostile father. In effect, the fantasy symbolically represented an attempt to allay the anxiety generated by an internalized father who had forbidden him to assert his natural "masculine strivings." The figure of a dominating woman seemed to represent composite aspects of both his mother and sister. By assuming the submissive, compliant stance he was reenacting both his mother's and his own humiliating role of a victim. In the sexualization of this scenario, however, he was also able to achieve some sense of mastery, control, and triumph by repetitively experiencing the trauma in a now pleasurable way through orgasm. Thus, he could reassure himself in this orgastic experience that he was sexually potent and masculine. Intrinsic in the fantasy was also his attempt at working through a revenge motive in which a sense of vindictive triumph was achieved. While he was being urinated upon, the women were also portrayed as being in a clearly bestial, undignified, and ultimately humiliating posture, betraying his underlying rage toward women. Hence, there were also sadistic elements in his overtly masochistic stance.

Throughout the course of treatment, the employment of transferential interpretations was crucial. In particular, when Mr E, who tended to initially idealize the therapist, felt misunderstood or rejected by him, the patient became significantly insecure, which resulted on several occasions in an increase in frequency of his deviant sexual fantasizing. The therapist interpreted this pattern in the light of the patient's experiences with his father. As the treatment proceeded, the therapist became a safer, new object in the patient's experience. Hence, this corrective experience allowed the patient to test out more assertive, heterosexual experiences that the patient was increasingly able to master. Accompanying this heterosexual assertiveness was the patient's increased sense of self-worth as an individual. During the subsequent course of treatment, the patient's perverse fantasy continued to recede in the background.

THE TRANSIENT SEXUALLY PERVERSE EXPERIENCE

Although it is difficult to document precisely, it is probable that most people have at one time or another transient sexually perverse experiences, most commonly in the form of fantasies. This is in accordance with the psychoanalytic observation that there is a latent perverse core in human nature traceable to earliest childhood sexual experiences before the advent of object genitality. This fantasized material that surfaces during the course of psychotherapy needs to be explored for its dynamic significance in the context of other prominent issues that are being dealt with in treatment, ie, the exploration of central characterological issues and the analysis of transference. Inasmuch as these fleeting perverse fantasies are more significant for what light they shed rather than representing a dysfunctional symptomatic problem, the therapist's emphasis is directed toward understanding their underlying meanings as well as the subjective impact they have on the patient. As such, there is no need for the therapist to attempt to intervene for the purpose of modifying these fantasies in a systematic and focused manner.

A clinical vignette illustrating the above is the following: A 29-year-old female whose boyfriend of a two-years' duration broke off their relationship in an abrupt and insulting manner, entered treatment because of dysphoric feelings and issues concerning self-esteem. She described on two recent occasions having had masturbatory fantasies of being sexually ravaged by a series of ugly and deformed men with huge penises while a bunch of jeering men looked on and masturbated. She was greatly distressed in having summoned up these fantasies and thereafter successfully suppressed them from occurring again. These fantasies served as an introduction for a discussion of her rage, humiliation, and sense of betrayal in her boyfriend's rejection and her attempts through disguised hostility to wreak revenge on him.

Analogs were explored in regard to earlier problematic relationships with men in her family history.

THE COMPULSIVE NONPARAPHILIAC SEXUALLY DISORDERED PATIENT

According to the DSM-III-R, this kind of problem is not a paraphiliac disorder, per se, but is categorized under 302.90 as a "Sexual Disorder Not Otherwise Specified." The sexuality is essentially "normative" but takes on an addictive or compulsive quality that the patient is unable to control. Examples of addictive sexuality abound in such forms as compulsive promiscuity, masturbation and use of pornography, engagement of prostitutes, and so forth. In contrast to paraphiliac individuals, compulsive sexually disordered persons are more likely to self-refer for treatment, and especially when their compulsive sexual behavior begins to markedly interfere in their lives. In recent years there has been an increase in the number and variety of 12-step-like self-help programs such as Sexaholic Anonymous and Sex and Love Anonymous. It is important to point out, however, that some of these sexually addicted individuals may also have accompanying paraphiliac tendencies and behaviors.

A clinical example is a 35-year-old married man with children employed in a middle-management capacity in a large corporation who has been having continual affairs over the years with women, mostly at his work place, and often juggling three or four of these affairs at one time. He came to psychotherapeutic treatment when his wife discovered his most recent affair and threatened to leave him. He disclosed in therapy a life-long pattern of compulsive womanizing that he acknowledged was getting increasingly out of control. In fact, he was terrified of contracting a sexually transmitted disease, especially AIDS. The strategy of treatment consisted of a focused dynamic exploration of the pattern and meaning of his sexual acting out. Additionally, several primary chains for covert sensitization, as well as stress-management techniques, were utilized. The affective-emotional roots underlying the behavior were traced to the sexualized patterns of interrelating in his earlier dysfunctional family, particularly with his hysterically seductive mother. Hence, his "Don Juan" complex was symptomatic of a kind of search for the unattainable mother as well as a statement of revenge directed against the same mother for having placed him in this perpetually dissatisfied position. Sexuality for him had clearly represented a form of narcissistic bliss, bolstering up his low self-esteem, as well as soothing anxiety, related to an insecure sense of self. Much of the therapeutic work centered on transferential usage of the therapist as the substituted self-object to help him cope with core anxiety-laden states.

FEMALE SEXUAL PERVERSIONS

Although sexually perverse behavior has been overwhelmingly identified with men, there is increasing awareness that deviant sexuality may exist as well in some women. It should be pointed out, however, that this area of deviant female sexuality remains to a large extent controversial as to its nature and incidence. As reported by the DMS-III-R, paraphilia is uncommonly diagnosed for females, except for masochism, in which the sexual ratio is estimated to be 20 males for each female. Certainly in the more extreme category of sex offenders, females comprise less than 2% of individuals who have managed to be processed through the criminal justice system.[1] The particular vulnerability of males to develop sexually perverse disorders had been reviewed in earlier sections of the book, and includes biological, psychodynamic, gender formation, and sociocultural issues.

Kaplan[2] has expanded the definition of sexually perverse disorders to "symbolically" include sexual areas of acting out such as kleptomania, anorexia, and the incest wife, and to relate the sexual perversion to caricatures of sociocultural versions of gender roles. Female perversions in this view parody feminine models of submission and purity. Also, if one includes such categories as compulsive sexual fantasizing and acting out in a more "normative" manner (promiscuity, "addictive" sexuality) the incidence of such perverse behavior is considerably more likely in females, as indicated by anecdotal clinical material. One may include in this category a certain percentage of female prostitutes. The acknowledgment in recent years of the so-called "love and romantic addiction" in the popular literature is another area that occurs among females and may overlap to some degree with problems related to the compulsive sexualization of interpersonal relationships.

It is generally known that females who have been sexually traumatized and abused are more likely to sexually act out and manifest symptoms of sexual dysfunctions.[3] One can speculate that a certain percentage of these individuals may manifest their difficulties in more "disguised" sexualized caretaking with their children. This would be consistent with the psychodynamic formulation that inappropriate maternal sexualized caretaking or overt sexual abuse of the child is aetiologically relevant to the formation of male sexual perversion. The developmental histories of these mothers may reveal a high incidence of personal sexual traumata and victimization, and consequent gender-related difficulties. The mothers' sexualized disorders may then be enacted in a more muted form as eroticized interactive patterns with their children. The children, in effect, become victims of the mothers' own unresolved victimization.

Specialized treatment of the female paraphiliac and sex offender patient has received scant attention because of the low incidence of the disorder, although it is very likely that there is an underreporting of the problem. This may be due to such factors (in the case of pedophilia) as the likelihood that the acts may be disguised as appropriate acts by the caretakers, the incestuous nature of the acts is less likely to be reported by a child dependent on his mother, and the misinterpretation by young boys of the incidents due to social learning.[1] It has been noted that women who have been involved in sexual abuse are often overcome by shame and guilt to the point where they are likely to leave treatment. Females who have been treated in specialized sex offenders programs have also manifested a marked degree of concomitant psychopathology. It may be that specialized attention needs to be focused on this population, although it is likely the women who seek treatment do so because of the symptomatology related to their own victimization. The sexual acting out is only disclosed in the course of therapy. As with male paraphilia, a broad-based and flexible bimodal approach would appear to be the most judicious treatment approach to take with this under-addressed population.

REFERENCES

1. Travin S, Cullen K, Protter B. Female sex offenders: severe victims and victimizers. *J Forensic Sci.* 1990;35:140–150.
2. Kaplan LJ. *Female Perversions.* New York, NY: Doubleday; 1991.
3. Becker JV, Skinner LJ, Abel GG, Tracey EC. Incidence and types of sexual dysfunctions in rape and incest victims. *J Sex Marital Ther.* 1984;10:185–192.

11

Summary and Conclusion

In recent years psychotherapists have become increasingly involved in the treatment of patients manifesting a wide array of sexually perverse disorders, ranging from transient sexual fantasies and urges through the mid- and moderate-range deviant sexual behaviors to the more severe paraphiliac disorders of an aggressive nature which include victims. The vast majority of sexually perverse individuals rarely come voluntarily to treatment specifically for the perverse disorder. The reasons for this avoidance of treatment are many, including the egosyntonic pleasure-producing quality of the symptom, the shame involved in disclosure, the fear (in cases where victims are involved) of their unlawful behavior being reported to the authorities, and their difficulty in finding therapists who specialize in treating these disorders. It is our impression that in a small percentage of cases, the individual may seek voluntary treatment for the sexual perversion. This happens because the sexual perversion has become dystonic, creating distress and dysfunction. He may experience anxiety, depression, somatic complaints, and interference in his relational life that is more or less directly attributable to the sexual perversion. In the specialized sex offender treatment area, virtually all patients are referred for treatment by third-party pressure (probation, parole, family court).

The clinician specializing in treating paraphiliac disorders is best equipped by having a full armamentarium of therapeutic skills. We have suggested an integrative approach to the problem primarily centering on a bimodal cognitive-behavioral—focused psychodynamic outlook. Patients presenting with deviant sexual difficulties can best be categorized as falling on a continuum that largely varies according to the level of self-control of the paraphiliac problem. At one end of the spectrum are individuals with the least self-control problems and the potential for victimizing others. They have to be most closely monitored in third-party arrangements, that is, probational or parole supervision. They also are more likely to present with deficits of impulse and a variety of other psychosocial deficiencies. The therapist must immediately place a greater emphasis on directive cognitive-behavioral interventions in order to extinguish the intensity of the sexual symptom. Also, it is likely that social rehabilitation in a more comprehensive manner needs to be addressed with these patients. Generally, psychodynamic intervention assumes a secondary role until the symptom abates.

At the other end of the spectrum are individuals presenting with mild perversions, that is, with symptoms of considerably less intensity and with less likelihood of harming victims. These individuals are less likely to be in a third-party supervisory arrangement, and they may require less monitoring. Psychodynamic intervention is likely to assume the bulk of the initial and continued treatment, centering on characterological issues with selective cognitive-behavioral interventions as needed.

Individuals on the mid-range of the continuum, require both the application of therapeutic tact and a continual reappraisal of the case in order to discriminatively utilize the appropriate "mixture" of components in the bimodal paradigm.

The initial focus of therapy can be schematized in the following way:

Mild perversion	*Severe perversion*
More self-control	Less self-control
Less deficits	More deficits
Two-party arrangement	Third-party monitoring-arrangement
Character-centered	Symptom-centered
Dynamic	Cognitive-behavioral

Summary and Conclusion

This characterization of sexual perversion is a generalization and serves only as a pragmatic guide. The clinician who has the full range of therapeutic skills can adapt his or her treatment plan more flexibly to meet the needs and problems of this challenging group of patients.

Index

Abstinence violation effect, 148
Addictive disorders, 122
Adult Self-Expression Scale, 128
AIDS
    public response to homosexuality, 30
Alcohol abuse
    as causal relationship of sexual offense, 84
    as disinhibiting factor, 84
    prior treatment of, 123
    sex offenders and, 83
American Humane Association
    American Association for Protecting Children (AAPC) of, 40
Androgenital syndrome, 76
Androgen insensitivity syndrome, 76
Androgen receptor defects, 76
Anterior pituitary gland, 76
Antiandrogen agents, 149
Antidepressant drug. See Prozac
Antiobsessional drug. See Serotonin
Assault Knowledge Inventory, 128
Assertiveness skills, 146
Assessment
    detailed sexual interview, 124–127
    penile plethysmography. See Penile plethysmography
    psychiatric interview, 122–123
    psychodynamic formulation, 127–128
    specialized testing, 128–129

Attitude
    rape myth acceptance, 128
Auditory cues
    audio-taped narratives, 129
    in penile plethysmographic assessment, 129
Aversive consequences, 143. See also Covert sensitization

Bandura's social learning theory. See Social learning process
Barr body, 75
Battered child syndrome, 387
Behavioral treatment,
    behavioral techniques, 27
    behaviorists and conscious fantasy production, 96
    cognitive-behavioral
Bestiality, 18
Bimodal integrative approach, 155, 157–158
Biological perspectives, 73–86
Bisexuality, 74
Brain damage
    aberrant sexual behavior, 80–82
    temporal lobe disorder in sexual behavior, 82
    temporal lobe epilepsy. See Psychomotor epilepsy
    temporal lobe syndrome. See Kluver-Bucy syndrome

Index

Buccal smear, 75

Castration anxiety, 102
Certificate of Confidentiality, 62
Chain in covert sensitization, 143, 169–171, 176, 180–181, 183
Chaining of behavior, 94
Child molestation, 37
Childhood fantasies, 44
Chromosome abnormalities
  gonadal dysgenesis, 76
  Klinefelter's syndrome, 76
  triple-X, 76
Clarke Sexual History Questionnaire for Males (SHQ), 128
Classical conditioning, 91–93
  conditional response (CR), 92
  conditional stimulus (CS), 92
  unconditional stimulus (UCS), 92
Classification of sexual perversion, 59–69. *See also Diagnostic and Statistical Manual* (DSM)
Clinical perspectives on prevalence, 43–49
Clomipramine, 86
Cognitive-behavioral
  approaches, 141–149, 155
  component of bimodal therapy, 158
  perspectives, 91, 97
  treatment program, 129
Cognitive distortions, 63, 97, 145
Cognitive factors, 96, 98
  direct cognitive influence, 96
  indirect cognitive influence, 96
Cognitive impairment. *See* Brain damage and aberrant sexual behavior
Cognitive restructuring, 145
Cognitive revolution, 95
Collated internal object, 108
Compulsive nonparaphiliac, 164, 190–191
Computed tomography scan measure, 81
Concretization of the symptom by acting it out, 160
Conscious fantasy. *See* Fantasies
Constructionistic sensibility, 95
Countertransference issues of, 14
Couples' therapy
  adjunctive couples' therapy, 152
  codependence, 152

Covert sensitization, 143–144
Criminologic data on sexual assaults, 38–43
  American Association for Protecting Children (AAPC), 40–41
  defining sex crimes, 40
  National Crime Survey (NCS), 42–43
  New York State Department of Correctional Services survey, 41–42
  New York State Divison of Criminal Justice Services survey, 41
  Uniform Crime Reporting (UCR) Program, 42
Critical period in developing central nervous system, 76
Cross-dressing. *See* Transvestism
Cyproterone acetate (CPA), 149–150

Dangerousness
  sex offender and, 31
  child molester and, 60
Depo-Provera. *See* Medroxyprogesterone acetate (MPA)
Depression and paraphiliac disorder, 84–85
Derogatis Sexual Functioning Inventory (DSFI), 128
Diagnostic and Statistical Manual
  DSM-I, 59
  DSM-II, 60
  DSM-III, 60
  DSM-III-R, 11, 62
Dionysius' festivals, 18
Disclosure in psychotherapy, 164, 174, 178, 182, 185
Drumstick-like appendage in the neotrophil, 75
Dyadic therapist–patient model, 14
Dynamic group therapy, 140
Dysfunctional family, 114, 151

Ego psychology, 137
Ellis' *Studies in the Psychology of Sex*, 24
Endogenous drive model of psychopathology, 104
Engulfment from the mother, 112
Erotic form of hatred, 105

Index

Erotic stimuli
  auditory erotic cues, 129
  in penile plethysmography, 129
  visual erotic cues, 129
Erection measurement studies. *See* Penile plethysmographic assessment
Ethical-forensic matters, 13
Exhibitionism, 48, 67, 85
  case of exhibitionism and voyeurism, 178–182

Family systems approach. *See* Treatment
Fantasies
  as distinguished from phantasy, 115
  conditioned sexual fantasy, 97
  dependent variable, 156
  independent variable, 156
  intervening variable, 156
  key fantasy and subsequent masturbation, 93
  perverse, 12
  prevalence among sex offenders, 63
  sexual perversion and, 115–116
  topographical levels (conscious, preconscious, unconscious), 96
Faulty gender-defined self identity, 105
Female penis concept, 112
Female sexual perversions, 164, 191–193
Fetishism, 83, 112
  See also Transvestic fetishism
Five (5) reductase deficiency, 76
Flagellation, 20
Fluoxetine, 85
Fluvoxamine, 86
Focused psychodynamic therapy, 157
  component of biomodal therapy, 159–161
  early psychoanalytic writings on, 160
  recently elaborated writings on, 160
Follicle-stimulating hormone (FSH), 78
Forensic psychiatry, 10
Forensic psychology, 10
Freud,
  original view of psychopathology, 101
  Three Essays on the Theory of Sexuality, 102
Frottage, 48

Gender development, 73–76
  biological factors, 73–78
  core gender identity, 74
  gender identity, 74
  gender role, 74
  gonadal steroids, 76
  prenatal factors, 75
Gender disturbances, 76–78
  Klinefelter's syndrome, 76, 77, 123
  Turner's syndrome, 76
Gender identity disorders, 61, 64
Gonadotropin-releasing hormone (GnRh), 78
Group psychotherapy with sex offender, 32, 136

Hermaphroditism, 74
Heterochromatic material, 75
Histocompatibility, 76
History of sexual perversion
  ancient Greek attitude, 17–35
  Augustine's position, 19
  colonial American attitude, 20
  early Christianity, 19
  early Middle Ages, 19
  early Romans, 18
  literary tradition, 19–20
  medico-psychiatric approach, 22–23
  modern legal-forensic considerations, 30–32
  modern perspectives, 17, 21–32
  Napoleonic Code, 21
  pederasty, 18
  premodern perspectives, 17, 18–21
  psychoanalytic approach, 26–27
  psychotechnologic approach, 27–28
  sexologic approach, 23–26
  sociopolitical approach, 28–30
  taboo, 17
  Victorianism, 19–20
Homosexuality
  ancient Greece, 18
  ego-dystonic homosexuality, 61, 64
  Gay Liberation groups, 29
Hypothalamic-pituitary-gonadal axis dysfunction, 79
Hysteric, 102

Incest
  childhood seduction, 43–45
  incestuous activity, 44, 49
  psychodynamic formulations, 114
  See also Child molestation; Pedophilia
Indeterminate sentences, 32
Interpersonal schools. See Psychodynamic perspectives
Interstitial cell-stimulating hormone. See Luteinizing hormone (LH)
Intrapsychic processes, 12

Karyotype, 77
Kluver-Bucy (temporal lobe) syndrome, 82
Kinsey reports, 24–26
Klinefelter's syndrome. See Gender disturbances
Krafft-Ebing's *Psychopathia Sexualis*, 22, 38

Learning behavior
  models of, 91
  Skinner's basic principles of, 92
Leitmotif, 160
Leydig cells, 76, 78
Luria-Nebraska Neuropsychological Battery, 81
Luteinizing hormone (LH), 78

Major affective disorder and paraphilia, 85
Manifest dream content, 160
Masochism
  clinical cases of sexually masochistic patients, 174–178, 185–189
  Leopold Von Sacher-Masoch, 20
  psychoanalytic conceptualization, 113
Masturbation, 13
  attitude of Victorians, 19
  excessive, 85
Masturbatory satiation, 144
Massachusetts Treatment Center
  Child Molester Typology One, Two, and Three, 66
  Rapist Typology One, Two, and Three, 66
Medroxyprogesterone actetate (MPA), 80, 135, 140

Mental retardation and deviant sexuality, 122
Mercury strain gauge, 129
Millon Clinical Multiaxial Inventory (MCMI), 129
Minnesota Multiphasic Personality Inventory (MMPI)-II, 129
Monitoring potential acting-out behavior
  two-party arrangement, 196
  third-party monitoring arrangement, 196
Multimodal integration, 161–162

Napoleonic Code. See History of sexual perversions
Narcissistic transference, 139
Nebraska Penal Code, 81
Negative operant consequence, 94
Neosexuality, 106
Nonparaphiliac sexual addictions, 85, 149
Nonprocreative sex, 20
Normative-based typologies, 60
North American Man/Boy Love Association (NAMBLA), 45

Object relationship, 110
Obsessive-compulsive disorder
  and paraphilia, 84
  sexual addiction, 85
Oedipus complex, 44, 101–102, 110–111
Operantly conditional response, 92
Oral sex, 13
Organic brain deficits. See Brain damage

Paraphilia Not Otherwise Specified, 64
Paraphiliac disorder
  mild type, 62, 164, 185–189
  moderate type, 164, 178–184
  severe type, 164–178
Participant modeling, 95
Pavlov's classical conditioning. See Classical conditioning
Pedophilia
  case of opposite sex, 167
  case of same sex, 165
  child molestation, 31, 37, 60, 65
  child sexual abuse, 31
  heterosexual pedophilia, 48

Index

Pedophilia (Cont.)
  homosexual pedophilia, 48
  psychodynamic considerations, 112
  sexual abuse, 31
Pedophile Cognition Scale, 128
Penile plethysmography
  circumferential (PCR), 129
  internal and external validity, 130
  limitations of, 131
  potential for abuse, 130–131
  volumetric (PVR), 129
Personality factors
  borderline individuals, 124
  characterological traits, 68
  personality disorders, 69, 122
  sex offenders, 67
Phallic women, 104
Phallometric testing. See Penile plethysmographic assessment
Phase-specific manifestations of sexual trauma. See Sexual trauma
Pornography
  excessive use of, 85
  sex offenders and, 98
Portal circulaton, 78
Positive operant consequence, 94
Postconviction stage, 63
Preconscious fantasy. See Fantasies
Preoedipal perversions, 110–111
  See also Socarides' classificatory system of sexual perversions
Prepared learning, 93
Prevalence rate of sexually perverse behavior, 37
Primitive gonads, 75
Protofeminity, 105
Prozac. See Fluoxetine
Psychodynamic perspectives
  classical and revisionistic views, 101–107
  contemporary pluralistic outlook, 109–111
  fantasy and sexual perversion. See Fantasies
  focused component of bimodal therapy, 157, 159–161
  relational schools, 107–109
  specific perversions, 111–114
Psychomotor epilepsy, 82

Psychosexual Disorders Not Elsewhere Classified, 61
Psychosis and deviant sexuality, 122
Puritanism, 20

Randomized Response Technique, 54
Rape
  antirape movement, 47
  heterosexual rape, 48
Rape crisis center
  emergency crisis intervention, 47
Rape trauma syndrome
  post-traumatic stress disorder, 47
Regional cerebral blood flow analysis, 81
Relapse prevention, 147–149
  abstinence (or rule) violation effect (AVE), 148
  cognitive restructuring antidote, 148
  high-risk situations (HRS), 148
  lapse, 148
  relapse, 148
Relational-structure model. See Psychodynamic perspectives

Sadism, 20–21
  Marquis de Sade, 20
Sadomasochistic
  fantasies, 37
  practices, 18
Schizoperversion, 110–111
  See also Socarides' classificatory system
Self-control techniques, 142–144
Self-object, 109
Self object transference. See Narcissistic transference
Self psychology. See Psychodynamic perspectives
Separation-individuation. See Psychodynamic perspectives
Sequelae of child sexual victimization, 43–48
Serotonin (5 hydroxytryptamine), 86
Sertoli cells, 79
Sex crimes, 40
Sex differences in the brain, 76
Sex education
  demystifying, 147

Sex education (*Cont.*)
  sexual dysfunctional disorders, 146–147
Sex offenders, 12
Sexual abusers, 12
Sexual addiction, 85
Sexual assault, 32
Sexual deviation, 61
  See also Paraphilia
Sexual dimorphism, 75
Sexual fantasies. *See* Fantasies
Sexual Interest Card Sort, 128
Sexual psychopathy
  defining condition of, 31
    Group for the Advancement of Psychiatry (GAP) report, 31
  sexual psychopath laws, 30–31
Sexual revolution, 30
Sexual trauma, 44–48
  phase-specific manifestations, 45–46
  See also Rape trauma syndrome
Sexuality, 17
Sexually perverse patients
  acting-out, 12
  benign, non–acting-out, 12
Short-term focused dynamic psychotherapy. *See* Focused psychodynamic therapy
Sick label, 14
Socarides' classificatory system of sexual perversions, 110–111
Social control
  agent of, 14
  sick label, 14
  sociocultural factors, 13
Social learning process. *See also* Learning behavior
  Bandura and, 92
  mental schemata and, 92
Social rehabilitative techniques, 145–146
Social skills teaching, 146
Specialized psychological testing. *See* Assessment
Specialized sex offender treatment programs, 136
Spermatorrhea, 23
Stereotaxic hypothalamotomic neurosurgery, 149

Stress management, 144–145
Substance abuse, 123
Surgical castration, 149
Survey data on sexual abuse, 49–54
  Kinsey survey, 50–54
  See also Kinsey reports
Symbolic modeling, 95

Taxonomy. *See* Typological considerations
Testosterone
  levels in sex offenders, 79–80
  production, 78
  relationship to sexual stimulation, 79–80
  testosterone-A-reductase, 80
Testicular determining factors (TDF), 75
Thorndike's Law of Effect, 92
Thought shifting, 142–143
Three Essays on the Theory of Sexuality. *See* Freud
Transient sexually perverse experience, 164, 189–190
Transitional object, 108
Transvestic fetishism, 182–184
Transvestism, 19, 77, 85
  Magnus Hirschfeld, 23
Traumatogenic seductive parent, 104
Treatment
  cognitive-behavioral, 141–147
  family systems, 150–152
  organic, 149–150
  psychodynamic, 136–141
  relapse prevention, 147–149
Turner's syndrome. *See* Gender disturbances
Twelve Steps of Alcoholics Anonymous. *See* Sexual addiction
Typological considerations, 65–67
  child molester typologies, 66
  rapist typologies, 66
  taxonomic systems, 65–67
  See also Classification of sexual perversion

Unconscious fantasy. *See* Fantasies
Unitary theory of sexual perversion, 105

Index

Vicarious learning, 95
Victimization. *See* Sequelae of child sexual victimization
Visual cues
 in penile plethysmographic assessments, 129
 series of slides, 129
Voyeurism
 Case of exhibitionism and voyeurism, 178–182

Wisconsin Sex Crimes Law, 68
Wolffian duct differentiation, 76

X Chromosome, 75

Y Chromosome, 74, 75

Zoophilia, 61, 64
 See also Bestiality